1 Operations with Whole Numbers

1. Find the sum of 4297 and 970 and the difference between them.

$$\begin{array}{r} {\scriptstyle 1\ \ 1} \\ 4297 \\ +\ \ \ 970 \\ \hline \end{array}$$
sum → 5267

$$\begin{array}{r} {\scriptstyle 3\ 12} \\ \cancel{4}297 \\ -\ \ \ 970 \\ \hline \end{array}$$
difference → 3327

2. Find the product of 296 and 4.

$$\begin{array}{r} {\scriptstyle 2} \\ 296 \\ \times\ \ \ \ 4 \\ \hline 4 \end{array}$$
↑
$6 \times 4 = 24$

→

$$\begin{array}{r} {\scriptstyle 3\ 2} \\ 296 \\ \times\ \ \ \ 4 \\ \hline 84 \end{array}$$
↑
$9 \times 4 + 2 = 36 + 2 = 38$

→

$$\begin{array}{r} {\scriptstyle 3} \\ 296 \\ \times\ \ \ \ 4 \\ \hline 1184 \end{array}$$ ← product
↑
$2 \times 4 + 3 = 8 + 3 = 11$

3. Find the quotient when 511 is divided by 7.

$$\begin{array}{r} 73 \\ 7\overline{)511} \\ 49 \\ \hline 21 \\ 21 \\ \hline \end{array}$$

73 ← quotient
49 ← $7 \times 7 = 49$
$51 - 49 = 2$ → 21 ← bring down 1
21 ← $7 \times 3 = 21$

(H)INTS:

- Align all numbers on the right hand side when doing vertical addition, subtraction and multiplication.

- In doing addition or multiplication, remember to carry groups of 10 to the column on the left if the sum or product of a column is greater than 10.

- In doing subtraction, borrow 10 from the column on the left if you can't take away.

- Continue to divide until the remainder is smaller than the divisor.

- Multiplication and division are done in order from left to right.

Find the answers mentally.

① $2 \times 7 \times 50$ = _____

② $5700 \div 10$ = _____

③ $5 \times 8 \times 20$ = _____

④ 2000×35 = _____

⑤ $5 \times 29 \times 2$ = _____

⑥ $27000 \div 300$ = _____

⑦ $1000 \times 20 \div 100$ = _____

⑧ $2 \times 62 \times 5$ = _____

⑨ $2000 \div 100 \times 5$ = _____

⑩ $30 \times 100 \div 10$ = _____

⑪ $500 \div 50 \times 100$ = _____

⑫ $400 \div 100 \times 10$ = _____

Do the calculation.

⑬ 2784 + 3796	⑭ 999 − 888
⑮ 2784 + 4370 − 401	⑯ 4983 + 3974 − 728

⑰ 595 ÷ 7	⑱ 314 x 8	⑲ 438 ÷ 6
⑳ 5) 3 2 5	㉑ 3) 8 7 3	㉒ 8) 7 3 6
㉓ 5 3 7 X 9	㉔ 8 5 4 X 6	㉕ 2 1 3 X 5

Find the answers.

㉖ The sum of seven thousand two and four hundred ninety-nine.

㉗ The difference between nine hundred eighty-four and five hundred seventy-eight.

Write your answers in the puzzle below.

ACROSS

A	7 x 30
B	208 ÷ 4
C	270 ÷ 9
D	30 x 69
E	48 ÷ 12
F	5 x 150

DOWN

A	225 ÷ 9
C	5 x 75
E	322 ÷ 7
F	19 x 4
G	366 ÷ 3

Do the division and write down the remainder in each case. The sum of the remainders is equal to the number of coconuts in the tree.

㉙ 218 ÷ 3   remainder = _____

㉚ 497 ÷ 7   remainder = _____

㉛ 100 ÷ 3   remainder = _____

㉜ 200 ÷ 5   remainder = _____

㉝ 124 ÷ 8   remainder = _____

㉞ 874 ÷ 4   remainder = _____

㉟ Sum of remainders   = _____

There are _____ coconuts in the tree.

Solve the problems. Show your work.

㊱   Jane is 7 years older than Jeff. Jane is 11 years old. How old is Jeff?

Jeff is _____ years old.

㊲   What is the perimeter of the rectangle?

```
              12 m
       ┌──────────────┐
2 m    │              │  2 m
       └──────────────┘
              12 m
```

㊳   Dan's heart beats 66 times a minute. How many times does it beat in an hour?

㊴   Farmer Fred's chickens lay 240 eggs per day. If he gets $2 for one dozen eggs, how much does he earn per day?

Solve the problems.

①   Write the next 3 numbers in each of the following sequences.

     a.   77   88   99   _____   _____   _____

     b.   72   84   96   _____   _____   _____

②   A number is divisible by 3 if the sum of its digits is divisible by 3. Circle the numbers which are divisible by 3. (Do not divide!)

     1234   5790   2927   9980   4563

Introducing Decimals

1. $0.94 = \dfrac{94}{100}$ or $\dfrac{9}{10} + \dfrac{4}{100}$ = 9 tenths and 4 hundredths

2. $0.4 = \dfrac{4}{10}$ or $\dfrac{40}{100}$ = 4 tenths or 40 hundredths

3. $0.02 = \dfrac{2}{100}$ = 2 hundredths

4. $1.43 = 1 + 0.43$

$\quad = 1 + \dfrac{43}{100}$

$\quad = 1$ and 43 hundredths

HINTS:

- ones → decimal point
  2.94 is a decimal number.
  tenths ↑ ↑ hundredths

- Read as two point nine four.

- 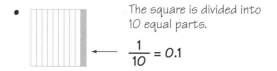 The square is divided into 10 equal parts.
  $\dfrac{1}{10} = 0.1$

- 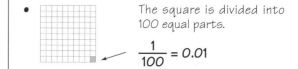 The square is divided into 100 equal parts.
  $\dfrac{1}{100} = 0.01$

- 1 tenth is the same as 10 hundredths.

- Deleting the zeros at the end of a decimal number will not affect the numerical value of a decimal number.
  $2.30 = 2.3$

- When rounding decimal numbers, round up if the last digit is 5 or more; otherwise, round down.

Complete the chart below.

	Decimal	Fraction
①	0.52	
②		$\dfrac{5}{100}$
③		$\dfrac{3}{10}$
④	0.09	
⑤		$7\dfrac{2}{10}$
⑥	4.1	

Place the numbers on the number line below.

⑦

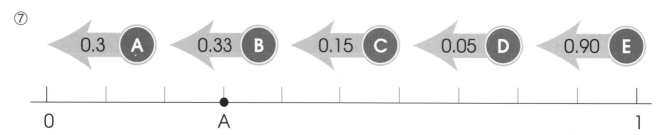

Write the numbers in order from least to greatest.

⑧   0.2, 0.15, 0.1, 0.02, 0.01

_____

⑨   1.45, 1.50, 1.4, 1.54, 1.05

_____

Write the numbers in order from greatest to least.

⑩   5.08, 5.80, 5.88, 0.58, 0.55, 0.50

_____

⑪   2.9, 2.09, 3.2, 2.39, 2.93, 2.3

_____

Write the quantities in decimal form.

⑫   5 cents = $ _____   ⑬   2 nickels = $ _____

⑭   3 quarters = $ _____   ⑮   4 dimes = $ _____

⑯   316 cm = _____ m   ⑰   37 mm = _____ cm

Write True (T) or False (F) in the (   ).

⑱   0.7 = 0.70   (   )   ⑲   1.02 = 1.2   (   )

⑳   3.0 = 3   (   )   ㉑   0.5 = .5   (   )

㉒ $9.1 = 9\frac{1}{100}$ (   )   ㉓ $2.3 = 2\frac{3}{100}$ (   )

Complete the expanded forms using decimals.

㉔ $7 + \frac{2}{100}$ = _____   ㉕ $3 + \frac{5}{10} + \frac{7}{100}$ = _____

㉖ $\frac{1}{10} + \frac{6}{100}$ = _____   ㉗ $2 + \frac{3}{10} + \frac{5}{100}$ = _____

Write an approximate decimal value for each of the numbers on the number line below.

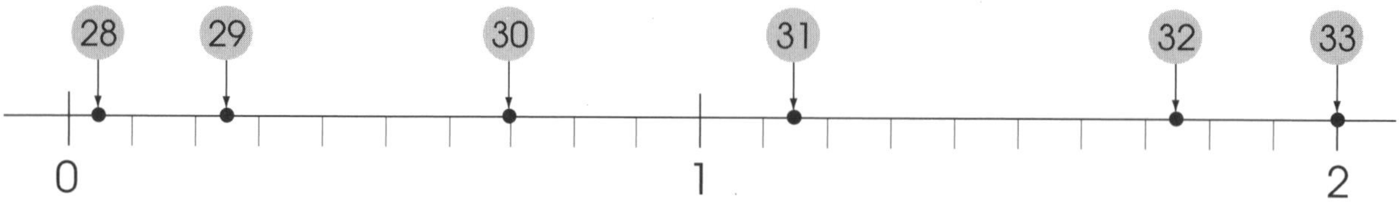

㉘ ________ ㉙ ________ ㉚ ________

㉛ ________ ㉜ ________ ㉝ ________

Write the place value and meaning of each underlined digit.

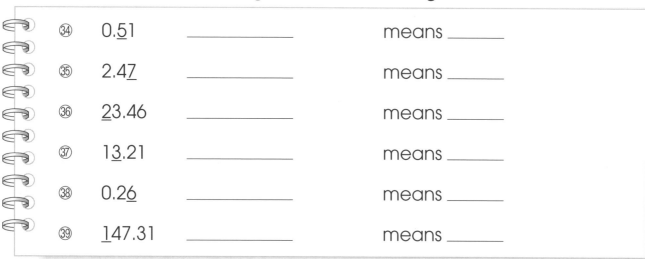

㉞ $0.\underline{5}1$ ________ means ________

㉟ $2.4\underline{7}$ ________ means ________

㊱ $\underline{2}3.46$ ________ means ________

㊲ $1\underline{3}.21$ ________ means ________

㊳ $0.2\underline{6}$ ________ means ________

㊴ $\underline{1}47.31$ ________ means ________

Round each of the following numbers to the nearest tenth.

㊵ 5.72 ________	㊶ 0.88 ________
㊷ 1.99 ________	㊸ 12.34 ________

Round each of the following numbers to the nearest hundredth.

㊹ 5.938 ________	㊺ 2.704 ________
㊻ 3.097 ________	㊼ 6.006 ________

Place < or > between each pair of decimal numbers.

㊽ 0.3 0.32	㊾ 0.09 0.9
㊿ 0.22 0.2	(51) 23.1 23.01

Answer the following questions.

(52) Ron finished a marathon race in 3 hours 57.8 minutes. John took 0.7 minutes longer.

a. How long did John take to finish the race? ____________

b. Did they both finish under 4 hours? ____________

(53) Ann spent $47.99 on a pair of jeans and $15.75 on a T-shirt. How much did she spend to the nearest dollar?

____

(54) Janice paid $0.80 for a chocolate bar. Write 2 different ways she could pay with 8 coins.

a. Use ____ 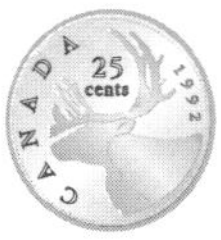

____ 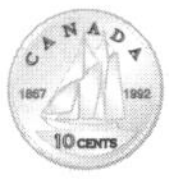

____ 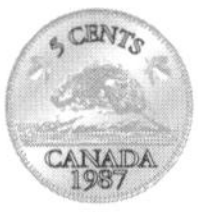

____ 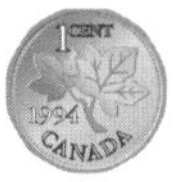

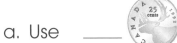

b. Use ____ 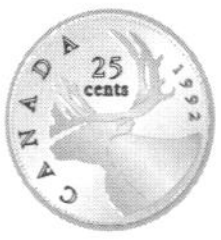

____ 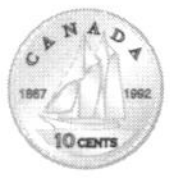

____ 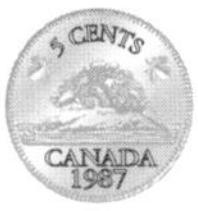

____ 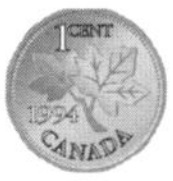

(55) Ming spent $195.55 at the mall. Write this amount in words.

____

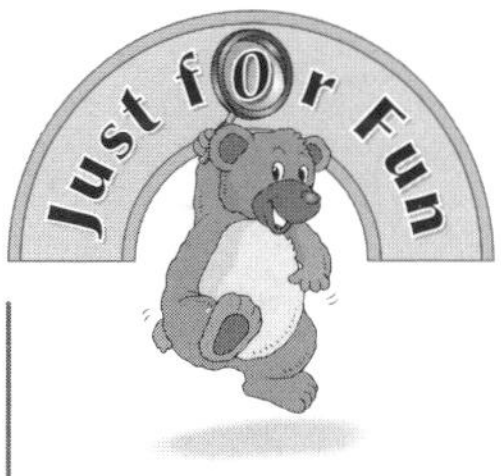

Determine the value for each symbol. Each symbol has a different value. Write down all the possible solutions.

■ = ________ ♠ = ________

◆ = ________ ♥ = ________

```
      ■ ◆ . 9
  + ♠ 8 . ♥
  ---------
    5 6 . 7
```

Adding Decimals

EXAMPLES

1. 57.23 + 85.9 + 0.78 + 30
    = 173.91

2. Write 219.57 in expanded form.
    219.57 = 200 + 10 + 9 + 0.5 + 0.07

align the decimal points
↓

```
  57.23
  85.90  ←
   0.78      write "0"
  30.00  ←   to fill the
 ───────     empty
 173.91      places
```

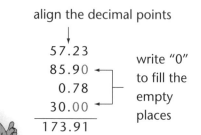

HINTS:

- Align the decimal points when doing vertical addition.
- Write zeros to fill the empty places.
- Add decimal numbers the same way we add whole numbers.
- Don't forget to add the decimal point in the answer.

Add these decimals in tenths.

①
$$\begin{array}{r} 0.7 \\ +\ 0.8 \\ \hline \end{array}$$

②
$$\begin{array}{r} 1.9 \\ +\ 8.7 \\ \hline \end{array}$$

③
$$\begin{array}{r} 30.2 \\ +\ 16.6 \\ \hline \end{array}$$

④
$$\begin{array}{r} 23.4 \\ +\ 41.6 \\ \hline \end{array}$$

⑤ 10.2 + 12.7 = _____

⑥ 0.9 + 12.8 = _____

Add these decimals in hundredths.

⑦
$$\begin{array}{r} 50.93 \\ +\ \ 7.28 \\ \hline \end{array}$$

⑧
$$\begin{array}{r} 6.54 \\ +\ 27.69 \\ \hline \end{array}$$

⑨
$$\begin{array}{r} 27.84 \\ +\ \ 3.07 \\ \hline \end{array}$$

⑩
$$\begin{array}{r} 100.30 \\ +\ \ \ 6.84 \\ \hline \end{array}$$

⑪ 5.83 + 3.0   = _____

⑫ 99.01 + 9.09   = _____

⑬ 5.50 + 0.9   = _____

⑭ 324.78 + 1.22 = _____

⑮ 123.45 + 34.56 = _____

⑯ 13.59 + 12.64 = _____

Add these decimals.

⑰ 5 + 7.8   = _____   ⑱ 5.9 + 0.78   = _____

⑲ 2.73 + 4.9   = _____   ⑳ 7 + 1.23   = _____

㉑ 5.9 + 8.73   = _____   ㉒ 5.03 + 2.9   = _____

㉓ 11.67 + 40.9   = _____   ㉔ 22.45 + 6.7   = _____

㉕ 52.93 + 109.2   = _____   ㉖ 809 + 2.82   = _____

㉗ 141.05 + 26.4   = _____   ㉘ 17.42 + 353   = _____

㉙ 0.98 + 3.2 + 12 = _____   ㉚ 9 + 61.4 + 45.5   = _____

㉛ 14.07 + 6.67 + 9.91   = _____

㉜ 4.5 + 2.77 + 1.82   = _____

㉝ 5 + 4.23 + 12.6   = _____

㉞ 4.97 + 9.3 + 1.87 + 5 = _____

㉟ 902 + 77.13 + 0.87   = _____

Write these decimals in expanded form.

㊱ 25.87 = _____

㊲ 12.93 = _____

Write the decimals.

㊳ 500 + 70 + 0.8 = _____

㊴ 100 + 8 + 0.6 + 0.04 = _____

Add the money. If the sum is larger than the amount in the previous question, write it on the line in ㊼ and add the sums to find Sally's savings.

㊵ $9.32 + $0.95 = ____________

㊶ $9.85 + $1.32 = ____________

㊷ $5.23 + $6.09 = ____________

㊸ $10.93 + $0.21 = ____________

㊹ $53.29 + $6.78 = ____________

㊺ $70.94 + $0.50 = ____________

㊻ $29.84 + $39.99 = ____________

㊼ ____

㊽ sum = ____________________________

㊾ Sally saves ________________ .

Do the following addition. Write + or – in the ◯ to show the relation of P, Q, R and S.

㊿ 5.9 + 12.8 = P ______

(51) 15.2 + 9.4 = R ______

(52) 19.4 + 3.9 = Q ______

(53) 7.8 + 9.6 = S ______

(54) P ◯ Q = R ◯ S

Solve the problems. Show your work.

55. Casla and Sally go to a movie. The tickets cost $5.50 each. Popcorn costs $3.75 and drinks cost $1.20 each. If they each have a drink and share the popcorn, how much do they pay altogether?

_____ = _____

They pay _____ altogether.

56. Ann's allowance in September is $6.75 the first week, $5.90 the second week, $6.50 the third week and only $5.00 the fourth week. How much does she get over the 4 week period?

57. Ron is training for triathlon. He cycles 25.2 km on Monday, 22.1 km on Wednesday, 24.8 km on Friday and 28.2 km on Saturday. How far does he cycle during the week?

Just for Fun

Bob has 17 coins. They are dimes, nickels and pennies. Their total value is $0.90. How many of each coin does he have?

Bob has _____ dimes, _____ nickels

and _____ pennies.

Subtracting Decimals

1. 29.43 − 17.86 = ?

$$
\begin{array}{r}
2\,9.\overset{3}{\cancel{4}}\overset{13}{\cancel{3}} \\
-\ 1\,7.8\,6 \\
\hline
7
\end{array}
\quad\rightarrow\quad
\begin{array}{r}
2\overset{8}{\cancel{9}}.\overset{13}{\cancel{4}}3 \\
-\ 1\,7.8\,6 \\
\hline
.5\,7
\end{array}
\quad\rightarrow\quad
\begin{array}{r}
2\overset{8}{\cancel{9}}.4\,3 \\
-\ 1\,7.8\,6 \\
\hline
1.5\,7
\end{array}
\quad\rightarrow\quad
\begin{array}{r}
2\,9.4\,3 \\
-\ 1\,7.8\,6 \\
\hline
1\,1.5\,7
\end{array}
$$

2. Jim ran 5.8 km and Andrea ran 7.25 km. How much farther did Andrea run?

7.25 − 5.8 = 1.45

$$
\begin{array}{r}
\overset{6}{\cancel{7}}.\overset{12}{\cancel{2}}\,5 \\
-\ \ 5.8\,0 \\
\hline
1.4\,5
\end{array}
$$

Andrea ran 1.45 km farther.

Hints:

- Align the decimal points when doing vertical subtraction.

- Write zeros to fill the empty places.

- Subtract decimal numbers the same way we subtract whole numbers.

- Use addition to check your answer.

- Don't forget to add the decimal point in the answer.

Subtract these decimals in tenths.

①
$$
\begin{array}{r}
0.7 \\
-\ \ 0.2 \\
\hline
\end{array}
$$

②
$$
\begin{array}{r}
5\,8.3 \\
-\ \ \ 1.8 \\
\hline
\end{array}
$$

③
$$
\begin{array}{r}
9.2 \\
-\ \ 2.9 \\
\hline
\end{array}
$$

④
$$
\begin{array}{r}
5.0 \\
-\ \ 3.8 \\
\hline
\end{array}
$$

⑤ 45.3 − 16.9 = _____

⑥ 72.4 − 38.6 = _____

Subtract these decimals in hundredths.

⑦
$$
\begin{array}{r}
1\,7.0\,4 \\
-\ 1\,2.0\,0 \\
\hline
\end{array}
$$

⑧
$$
\begin{array}{r}
1.5\,7 \\
-\ \ 0.8\,8 \\
\hline
\end{array}
$$

⑨
$$
\begin{array}{r}
8.0\,4 \\
-\ \ 4.9\,8 \\
\hline
\end{array}
$$

⑩ 704.23 − 125.07 = _____

⑪ 32.16 − 8.45 = _____

Subtract these decimals.

⑫ 2.0 – 0.02 = _____   ⑬ 9.03 – 4 = _____

⑭ 7.9 – 4.13 = _____   ⑮ 10.4 – 2.13 = _____

⑯ 8.1 – 5.08 = _____   ⑰ 15 – 3.62 = _____

⑱ 12.1 – 4.23 = _____   ⑲ 9.5 – 7.68 = _____

⑳ 0.96 – 0.08 = _____   ㉑ 0.72 – 0.5 = _____

㉒ 1.1 – 0.84 = _____   ㉓ 2.3 – 1.49 = _____

㉔ 0.26 – 0.26 = _____   ㉕ 0.36 – 0.3 = _____

㉖ 42.1 – 9.63 = _____   ㉗ 98 – 71.6 = _____

㉘ 206.37 – 55.6 = _____   ㉙ 58.9 – 8.9 = _____

㉚ 42.48 – 22.7 = _____   ㉛ 1200 – 1000.6 = _____

Round each of the following differences to the nearest whole number.

㉜ 8.4 – 5.7 = _____   ㉝ 3.1 – 1.7 = _____

㉞ 58.9 – 19.2 = _____   ㉟ 14.2 – 5.4 = _____

㊱ 22.4 – 8.9 = _____   ㊲ 36.4 – 22.8 = _____

Round each of the following differences to the nearest tenth.

㊳ 9.23 – 6.57 = _____   ㊴ 7.63 – 5.87 = _____

㊵ 28.97 – 17.85 = _____   ㊶ 32.04 – 13.68 = _____

㊷ 45 – 10.73 = _____   ㊸ 19.4 – 6.83 = _____

Complete the number sentences and colour the boxes containing your answers in the number chart below.

(44) 9.2 – 7.8 = ________

(45) 9.3 – ________ = 1.3

(46) 9.23 – 5.87 = ________

(47) 8.2 – ________ = 5.8

(48) 5.2 + ________ = 7.1

(49) 3 – 0.39 = ________

(50) 2 + 3 – 0.8 = ________

(51) 5.2 – 3.97 = ________

(52) ________ – 2.3 = 4.7

(53) 5 + ________ + 2.3 = 7.9

(54) 15 – ________ = 7.3

(55) 9.37 – 1.99 = ________

(56) 27.62 – 13.49 = ________

(57) 12.13 – ________ = 2.67

(58)

11.4	7.7	7.38	7.0	6.94
17.0	5.8	1.4	10.6	9.17
7.5	0.2	14.13	5.2	3.61
15.1	9.3	4.2	14.0	15.2
14.8	3.63	9.46	41.11	12.3
12.3	22.3	2.61	2.60	11.36
2.63	0.6	8.0	1.23	3.27

(59) What is the letter formed by the coloured boxes?

The letter formed by the coloured boxes is ________ .

Solve the problems. Show your work.

60   Bill pays $35 for his groceries. How much change does he get if the total is $32.85?

   _____ = _____

   He gets _____ change.

61   Sue weighs 45.2 kg. Her sister weights 41.5 kg. How much heavier is Sue than her sister?

62   The CN Tower in Toronto is 0.55 km high. The Calgary Tower is 0.19 km high. How much taller is the CN Tower?

63   At a high school track meet, Ben ran 100 m in 11.87 seconds and Carl ran the same distance in 12.13 seconds. How much longer did Carl take?

Just for Fun

Fill in the missing numbers in the magic square. All numbers from 1 to 9 must be used.

In a magic square, the sum of the numbers in a row, column or diagonal is the same.

	9	
3		7
8	1	

5 More Addition and Subtraction of Decimals

1. 5.93 + 17.29 − 3.74   or
   = 23.22 − 3.74
   = 19.48

   5.93 + 17.29 − 3.74
   = 5.93 − 3.74 + 17.29 ← order of operations changed
   = 2.19 + 17.29
   = 19.48 ← still the same answer

2. 2 − 3.1 + 1.93
   = 2 + 1.93 − 3.1 ← Order of operations is changed because you can't take away 3.1 from 2.
   = 3.93 − 3.1
   = 0.83

$$\begin{array}{r} 2.00 \\ +\ 1.93 \\ \hline 3.93 \end{array} \qquad \begin{array}{r} 3.93 \\ -\ 3.10 \\ \hline 0.83 \end{array}$$

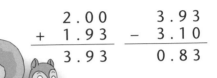

Find the answers mentally.

① 5.2 − 3.2 + 17.5   = _____

② 3.75 − 1.25 − 0.5   = _____

③ 5.99 − 3.99 + 4.99   = _____

④ 12 − 0.5 + 2.5   = _____

⑤ 7.55 + 3.45 − 0.50   = _____

⑥ 3 − 0.75 − 0.75   = _____

⑦ 1.9 − 0.5 − 1.4   = _____

⑧ 9.99 + 10.01 − 5.00   = _____

⑨ 13.25 − 5.5 + 2.25   = _____

⑩ 26.5 − 2 + 3.5   = _____

⑪ 45.85 − 70.5 + 25.15   = _____

⑫ 175.5 − 155.5 − 2.5   = _____

⑬ 115.50 − 100.00 − 5.50   = _____

⑭ 125.75 + 25.25 − 51.0   = _____

HINTS:

- To change the order of operations in multi-step operations, move the number together with the sign immediately in front of it.

  e.g.   5.1 + 3.2 − 4.9
       = 5.1 + 4.9 − 3.2
       = 10 − 3.2
       = 6.8 ✗

       5.1 + 3.2 − 4.9
       = 5.1 − 4.9 + 3.2
       = 0.2 + 3.2
       = 3.4 ✓

- Remember to add zeros for missing decimal places in vertical addition or subtraction.

Find the answers. Show your work.

⑮ 19.2 – 3.75

= _____

⑯ 7 – 3.72

= _____

⑰ 22 – 3.5 – 9.7

= _____

⑱ 7.1 + 3 – 5.09

= _____

⑲ 1 – 0.09 + 3.78

= _____

⑳ 7.3 + 2.9 – 5.4

= _____

㉑ 123.55 – 17.55 + 3.25

= _____

㉒ 125 – 100.95 – 3.72

= _____

㉓ 197.8 + 188.7 – 142.9

= _____

㉔ 1000 – 1.2 + 5.00

= _____

㉕ 0.09 + 0.92 – 0.08

= _____

㉖ 77 + 29.2 – 5.93

= _____

㉗ 26.94 – 47.86 + 35.48

= _____

㉘ 6.73 – 28.45 + 32.38

= _____

Show your work for the following money problems.

㉙ $12.23 + $7.00 − $3.79

= _____

㉚ $100.00 − $7.55 − $19.35

= _____

㉛ $59.70 − $32.90 − $2.00

= _____

㉜ $100.00 − $3.50 + $1.50

= _____

㉝ $10.00 + 0.79 − $0.55

= _____

㉞ $15.25 − $6.75 + $3.02

= _____

Round each answer to the nearest cent.

㉟   59.7¢ − 3.9¢ + 2.8¢

= _____

㊱   39.8¢ − 5.2¢ − 1.3¢

= _____

㊲   120.1¢ + 9.8¢ − 108.2¢

= _____

㊳   0.9¢ + 0.7¢ + 5.3¢

= _____

Fill in the missing number in each of the following number sentences.

㊴   12.3 − ☐ + 1.7 = 5.9

㊵   0.23 + ☐ = 1.90

㊶   25.3 − 19.8 + ☐ = 7.0

㊷   ☐ − 7.8 = 12.2

㊸   ☐ + 15.77 − 8.69 = 7.73

㊹   12.51 − ☐ = 9.07

Solve the problems. Show your work.

45 Sam has saved $25.00 for a trip to town. He spends $4.55 on transportation and $6.99 on lunch. How much does he have left?

_____ = _____

He has _____ left.

46 Rebecca earns $35.00 from a baby-sitting job. She uses the money to buy gifts for Clara and Debbie. Clara's gift costs $5.95 and Debbie's gift costs $17.45. How much does Rebecca have left?

47 Adam, Bob & Colin went to the CNE together. The fare cost them $6.50 each and a 1-day pass cost $19.95 each. Lunch cost $7.50 each and they each had a discount coupon worth $2.00. How much did each of them spend?

48 Penny, Peter and Pam contribute $17.50 each to buy a birthday gift for Sue. They decide to buy 2 CDs which cost $20.95 each. The tax for 2 CDs is $6.30. Do they have enough money?

Answer Sally's question.

If you put 1¢ in your piggy bank on Monday, 2¢ on Tuesday, 4¢ on Wednesday, 8¢ on Thursday and so on, how much will you have saved at the end of 1 week?

_____

Multiplying Decimals by Whole Numbers

6

EXAMPLES

1. 7.3 x 9 = 65.7

$$\begin{array}{r} \overset{2}{7}.3 \\ \times \quad 9 \\ \hline 6\,5.7 \end{array}$$

7.3 ← 1 decimal place

x 9 ← align the numbers

6 5 . 7 ← 1 decimal place in product

2. Danielle buys 5 books at $5.95 each. How much does she pay altogether?

$5.95 x 5 = $29.75

She pays $29.75 altogether.

$$\begin{array}{r} \overset{4}{5}.\overset{2}{9}5 \\ \times \quad 5 \\ \hline 2\,9.75 \end{array}$$

5 . 9 5 ← 2 decimal places

x 5 ← align the numbers

2 9 . 7 5 ← 2 decimal places in product

3. 0.75 x 10 = 7.5 ← move the decimal point one place to the right

4. 0.75 x 100 = 75. ← move the decimal point two places to the right

HINTS:

- Align all numbers on the right hand side.

- Multiply the decimals as with whole numbers, from right to left.

- The number of decimal places in the product is the same as that in the question.

- Multiplying a decimal number

  by 10 → move the decimal point one place right

  by 100 → move the decimal point two places right

  and so on.

- Check if your answer is reasonable by rounding the decimal to the nearest whole number and estimate the answer.

Find the products mentally.

① 0.2 x 5 = _____

② 3.2 x 10 = _____

③ 0.1 x 7 = _____

④ 0.01 x 8 = _____

⑤ 3.0 x 4 = _____

⑥ 1.1 x 9 = _____

⑦ 4.01 x 6 = _____

⑧ 5.4 x 100 = _____

⑨ 9.15 x 10 = _____

⑩ 0.01 x 10 = _____

⑪ 0.1 x 100 = _____

⑫ 9.3 x 10 = _____

⑬ 100.4 x 2 = _____

⑭ 0.08 x 100 = _____

⑮ 0.62 x 10 = _____

⑯ 0.1 x 10 = _____

⑰ 24.8 x 10 = _____

⑱ 0.01 x 100 = _____

Write the decimal point in each product.

⑲ $\begin{array}{r} 4.7 \\ \times \quad 3 \\ \hline 1\,4\,1 \end{array}$	⑳ $\begin{array}{r} 2.6\,9 \\ \times \qquad 4 \\ \hline 1\,0\,7\,6 \end{array}$	㉑ $\begin{array}{r} 1\,0.9 \\ \times \qquad 5 \\ \hline 5\,4\,5 \end{array}$

㉒ $6.47 \times 7 = 4\,5\,2\,9$	㉓ $5.55 \times 8 = 4\,4\,4\,0$

Find the products. Show your work.

㉔ $\begin{array}{r} 7.3 \\ \times \quad 9 \\ \hline \end{array}$	㉕ $\begin{array}{r} 4.9 \\ \times \quad 7 \\ \hline \end{array}$	㉖ $\begin{array}{r} 1\,2.2 \\ \times \qquad 8 \\ \hline \end{array}$
㉗ $\begin{array}{r} 5.7\,2 \\ \times \qquad 5 \\ \hline \end{array}$	㉘ $\begin{array}{r} 9.8\,9 \\ \times \qquad 6 \\ \hline \end{array}$	㉙ $\begin{array}{r} 2.7 \\ \times \quad 4 \\ \hline \end{array}$
㉚ $\begin{array}{r} 0.9\,8 \\ \times \qquad 4 \\ \hline \end{array}$	㉛ $\begin{array}{r} 4.8\,3 \\ \times \qquad 7 \\ \hline \end{array}$	㉜ $\begin{array}{r} 0.1\,8 \\ \times \qquad 9 \\ \hline \end{array}$
㉝ $\begin{array}{r} 3.2\,5 \\ \times \qquad 9 \\ \hline \end{array}$	㉞ $\begin{array}{r} 1.3\,8 \\ \times \qquad 7 \\ \hline \end{array}$	㉟ $\begin{array}{r} 2.9 \\ \times \quad 8 \\ \hline \end{array}$
㊱ $\begin{array}{r} 7\,2.3 \\ \times \qquad 7 \\ \hline \end{array}$	㊲ $\begin{array}{r} 9.9\,9 \\ \times \qquad 3 \\ \hline \end{array}$	㊳ $\begin{array}{r} 0.7\,6 \\ \times \qquad 6 \\ \hline \end{array}$

Estimate. Then find the exact products.

		Estimate	Exact Product
㊴	5.2 x 7		
㊵	3.7 x 2		
㊶	9.81 x 5		
㊷	8.23 x 6		
㊸	3.75 x 3		
㊹	0.36 x 8		
㊺	0.17 x 9		
㊻	8.44 x 4		

Check the answers of the following multiplication. Put a ✓ in the box if the answer is correct; otherwise, write the correct answer in the box.

㊼

$$\begin{array}{r} 2.31 \\ \times \quad 6 \\ \hline 1.386 \end{array}$$

☐

㊽

$$\begin{array}{r} 0.02 \\ \times \quad 5 \\ \hline 0.10 \end{array}$$

☐

㊾

$$\begin{array}{r} 1.03 \\ \times \quad 3 \\ \hline 3.9 \end{array}$$

☐

Fill in the boxes.

㊿ 7.15 x ☐ = 715

(51) 5.1 x ☐ = 15.3

(52) ☐ x 3.2 = 32

(53) ☐ x 0.9 = 90

(54) $\frac{\square}{10} = 15.9$

(55) $\frac{\square}{3} = 10.3$

Solve the problems. Show your work.

⑤⑥ Sina buys 3 CDs at $23.99 each. How much does she pay altogether?

_____ = _____

She pays _____ altogether.

⑤⑦ Ron buys 4 trees at $89.50 each. Calculate the total cost.

⑤⑧ Adam walks 2.3 km each day to school. How far does he walk in a 5 day week?

⑤⑨ How much space do 8 textbooks occupy on a book shelf if each is 3.2 cm thick?

⑥⓪ Susanne buys 3 T-shirts at $12.95 each and 2 pairs of jeans at $39.99 each. How much does she pay altogether to the nearest dollar?

Help Bob solve the problem.

How can I add four + signs in the following number sentence to make it true?

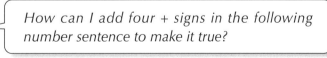

4   4   4   4   4   4   4   4   =   500

Dividing Decimals by Whole Numbers

1. $5.7 \div 3 = 1.9$

$$3\overline{)5.7} \longrightarrow \begin{array}{r} 1 \\ 3\overline{)5.7} \\ \underline{3} \\ 2 \end{array} \longrightarrow \begin{array}{r} 1 \\ 3\overline{)5.7} \\ \underline{3\downarrow} \\ 27 \end{array} \longrightarrow \begin{array}{r} 1.9 \\ 3\overline{)5.7} \\ \underline{3} \\ 27 \\ \underline{27} \end{array}$$

divisor — 3

dividend — 5.7

quotient — 1.9

2. $6.2 \div 4 = 1.55$

$$4\overline{)6.2} \longrightarrow \begin{array}{r} 1 \\ 4\overline{)6.2} \\ \underline{4\downarrow} \\ 22 \end{array} \longrightarrow \begin{array}{r} 1.5 \\ 4\overline{)6.2} \\ \underline{4} \\ 22 \\ \underline{20} \\ 2 \end{array} \longrightarrow \begin{array}{r} 1.5 \\ 4\overline{)6.20} \\ \underline{4} \\ 22 \\ \underline{20\downarrow} \\ 20 \end{array} \longrightarrow \begin{array}{r} 1.55 \\ 4\overline{)6.20} \\ \underline{4} \\ 22 \\ \underline{20} \\ 20 \\ \underline{20} \end{array}$$

add extra zero

3. $7.5 \div 10 = 0.75$

move the decimal point one place to the left

4. $7.5 \div 100 = 0.075$

move the decimal point two places to the left

Find the quotients mentally.

① $9.8 \div 10$ = _____

② $0.32 \div 10$ = _____

③ $75.0 \div 100$ = _____

④ $9.2 \div 1000$ = _____

⑤ $3.28 \div 10$ = _____

⑥ $0.05 \div 100$ = _____

⑦ $0.08 \div 10$ = _____

⑧ $154.93 \div 100$ = _____

⑨ $316.45 \div 100$ = _____

HINTS:

- Divide the decimals as with whole numbers, from left to right.

- If there is a remainder, add zeros to the right of the dividend after the decimal point. Continue to divide until the remainder is zero or you have enough decimal places.

- Don't forget to put a decimal point in the quotient above the one in the dividend.

- Always check if your answer makes sense.
  e.g. $6 \div 3 = 2$
  so $5.7 \div 3 = 1.9$ is reasonable.

- Dividing a decimal number
  by 10 ⟶ move the decimal point one place left.
  by 100 ⟶ move the decimal point two places left
  and so on.

Write the decimal point in each quotient. Add zeros where necessary.

⑩ $52.8 \div 3$ =   1 7 6   ⑪ $0.84 \div 7$ =   1 2

⑫ $14.28 \div 7$ =   2 0 4   ⑬ $2.08 \div 4$ =   5 2

Find the quotients. Show your work.

⑭ $7\overline{)8.05}$	⑮ $9\overline{)66.6}$	⑯ $7\overline{)73.5}$
⑰ $6\overline{)0.852}$	⑱ $4\overline{)0.24}$	⑲ $8\overline{)160.8}$
⑳ $3\overline{)12.09}$	㉑ $5\overline{)52.65}$	㉒ $8\overline{)36.4}$
㉓ $4\overline{)70.4}$	㉔ $5\overline{)10.4}$	㉕ $9\overline{)19.35}$

Divide. Show your work. Match the letters with the numbers in the boxes. What is the message?

㉖ Ⓘ $4\overline{)9.2}$	㉗ Ⓐ $3\overline{)0.57}$	㉘ Ⓣ $2\overline{)5.1}$
㉙ Ⓔ $7\overline{)35.84}$	㉚ Ⓣ $5\overline{)760.5}$	㉛ Ⓛ $5\overline{)35.05}$
㉜ Ⓡ $8\overline{)10.4}$	㉝ Ⓢ $7\overline{)380.1}$	㉞ Ⓟ $4\overline{)503.4}$
㉟ Ⓣ $5\overline{)0.45}$	㊱ Ⓛ $9\overline{)58.77}$	㊲ Ⓢ $6\overline{)502.38}$

㊳   What does Sally see in the night sky?

7.01	2.3	2.55	152.1	6.53	5.12

54.3	0.09	0.19	1.3	83.73

Solve the problems. Show your work.

③⑨ John mails 10 equal packages. The total weight is 32.5 kg. How much does each package weigh ?

_____ = _____

Each package weighs _____ .

④⓪ On his summer holidays Bob drove 7350 km in 100 hours. How far did he travel each hour?

④① Sam divides 36.4 metres of phone cable into 8 equal parts. How long is each part?

④② 8 students share the cost of a trip. If the total cost of the trip is $394.00, how much does each student pay?

④③ An equilateral triangle has all sides equal. If the perimeter is 13.5 cm, what is the length of each side?

Look for the pattern. What are the next 3 numbers?

1 , 1 , 2 , 3 , 5 , 8 , 13 , , ,

More Multiplying and Dividing of Decimals

8

EXAMPLES

1. 7.92 × 5 = 39.6

$$
\begin{array}{r}
{\scriptstyle 4\ 1} \\
7.9\,2 \\
\times\quad 5 \\
\hline
3\,9.6\,\cancel{0}
\end{array}
$$
← delete the zero at the last decimal place

put a zero in the quotient

2. 10.25 ÷ 5 = 2.05

$$
\begin{array}{r}
2.5 \\
5\,\overline{)10.25} \\
10 \\
\hline
25 \\
25 \\
\hline
\end{array}
$$
✗

$$
\begin{array}{r}
2.05 \\
5\,\overline{)10.25} \\
10 \\
\hline
25 \\
25 \\
\hline
\end{array}
$$
✓

Find the answers mentally.

HINTS:

- The number of decimal places in the product is the same as that in the question, but a zero at the last decimal place can be deleted.

  e.g. 7.92 × 5 = 39.6 ←

  only one decimal place in the product because the zero in the hundredths place is deleted

- Remember to put a zero in the quotient when the dividend is smaller than the divisor.

  e.g. 10.25 ÷ 5 = 2.05   but not 2.5

  a zero is put at the tenths place because 2 in the dividend is smaller than the divisor 5

① 7.34 × 10 = _____

② 9.23 ÷ 10 = _____

③ 123.4 ÷ 100 = _____

④ 2.42 ÷ 2 = _____

⑤ 36.9 ÷ 3 = _____

⑥ 1.2 × 100 = _____

⑦ 0.15 ÷ 5 = _____   ⑧ 80.8 ÷ 8 = _____

⑨ 342.9 ÷ 100 = _____   ⑩ 34.29 × 1000 = _____

⑪ 1.25 × 100 = _____   ⑫ 0.02 ÷ 10 = _____

⑬ 0.4 × 10 = _____   ⑭ 1.18 × 10 = _____

⑮ 0.04 × 100 = _____   ⑯ 1.25 ÷ 100 = _____

⑰ 0.02 × 10 = _____   ⑱ 63.5 × 10 = _____

Do the calculation. Show your work.

⑲
$$4\overline{)94.4}$$

⑳
$$7\overline{)7.28}$$

㉑
$$3\overline{)45.09}$$

㉒
$$\begin{array}{r} 3.92 \\ \times\quad 4 \\ \hline \end{array}$$

㉓
$$\begin{array}{r} 10.3 \\ \times\quad 7 \\ \hline \end{array}$$

㉔
$$\begin{array}{r} 5.91 \\ \times\quad 6 \\ \hline \end{array}$$

㉕
$$6\overline{)7.92}$$

㉖
$$9\overline{)17.1}$$

㉗
$$5\overline{)6.2}$$

㉘
$$\begin{array}{r} 0.47 \\ \times\quad 8 \\ \hline \end{array}$$

㉙
$$\begin{array}{r} 18.2 \\ \times\quad 9 \\ \hline \end{array}$$

㉚
$$\begin{array}{r} 36.7 \\ \times\quad 2 \\ \hline \end{array}$$

Find the answers.

㉛ 1.25×8 = _____

㉜ 1.75×4 = _____

㉝ $1.19 \div 7$ = _____

㉞ $10.4 \div 4$ = _____

㉟ 3.08×9 = _____

㊱ $76.8 \div 3$ = _____

㊲ $89 \times 10 \div 10$ = _____

㊳ $1.9 \times 10 \times 10$ = _____

Estimate. Then complete only those questions with a product greater than 15.

㊴	㊵	㊶
7 . 2 X 2	7 . 9 X 2	3 . 8 X 4
㊷	㊸	㊹
1 . 9 X 9	3 . 1 X 5	0 . 2 5 X 1 0

Estimate. Then complete only those questions with a quotient smaller than 2.

㊺	㊻	㊼
9) 1 2 . 6	3) 7 . 2	1 0) 2 3 . 4
㊽	㊾	㊿
3) 5 . 7	6) 1 0 . 8	7) 1 3 . 3

Fill in the blanks.

㉜ 12.7 ÷ _____ = 0.127

㉝ 3.92 X _____ = 39.2

㉞ _____ ÷ 3 = 1.14

㉟ 5.8 X _____ = 11.6

㊱ 2 X _____ = 12.4

㊲ _____ ÷ 7 = 1.3

㊳ 0.18 X _____ = 18

㊴ 54 ÷ _____ = 5.4

Answer the questions. Show your work.

⑤⑨ The Grade 5 class collects $58.20 to buy gifts for 3 children in a needy family. How much can they spend on each gift if the money is divided evenly?

_____ = _____

They can spend _____ on each gift.

⑥⓪ Mrs Ling buys plants for her patio. She buys 3 plants at $19.95 each, 2 plants at $12.45 each and 10 plants at $1.25 each. How much does she pay altogether?

⑥① 5 friends buy 2 pizzas at $12.99 each, 2 cans of juice at $1.29 each and 2 packets of chips at $1.49 each. They divide the total cost among them. How much must they each pay? Give the answer to the nearest cent.

⑥② Carol is buying food for her dog. She can buy a 3 kg bag for $29.40 or a 5 kg bag for $39.50. Calculate the cost per kg for each bag. Which is the better buy?

What number am I?

I am a decimal number. Multiply me by 35. Divide the product by 7. The result is 2.5.

_____

Midway Review

Answer the questions. Show your work.

① 3.75 + 4.2 + 11 = _____	② 13.04 − 2.87 + 1.59 = _____
③ 8.4 × 8 = _____	④ 8.4 ÷ 8 = _____
⑤ 3 × 5.42 = _____	⑥ 5.58 ÷ 9 = _____
⑦ 26.13 × 8 = _____	⑧ 9.6 ÷ 3 = _____

Help Sally put the digits and decimal point in the right order to solve the problems.

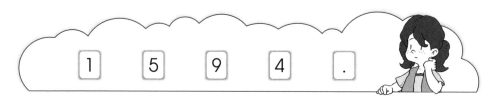

⑨ The largest decimal number with one decimal place _____

⑩ The smallest decimal number with two decimal places _____

⑪ The sum of the two decimals in ⑨ and ⑩ _____

⑫ The smallest decimal number with one decimal place and 9 at the ones place _____

⑬ The largest decimal number with two decimal places and 9 at the hundredth place _____

⑭ The difference of the two decimals in ⑫ and ⑬ _____

Complete the chart.

	Number	Number x 10	Number ÷ 10
⑮	52.0		
⑯	0.7		
⑰	0.12		
⑱		75.0	
⑲		3.0	
⑳			0.8
㉑			15.0

Circle the letter which represents the correct answer to each problem.

㉒　John earns $15.00 per hour.　He works 9 hours a day, 5 days a week. How much does he earn per week?

    A. $135.00　　　B. $630.00　　　C. $450.00　　　D. $675.00

㉓　If $1.00 U.S. is worth $1.50 Canadian, how much is $7.00 U.S. worth in Canadian money?

    A. $8.50　　　B. $4.75　　　C. $10.50　　　D. $7.35

㉔　Mrs Wing earns 1.5 times her regular hourly wage on Sundays.　She earns $8.00 per hour on weekdays.　How much is her hourly wage on Sundays?

    A. $6.00　　　B. $10.00　　　C. $12.00　　　D. $16.00

㉕　John reads 10 pages per hour.　How many pages does he read in 2.5 hours?

    A. 20　　　B. 22.5　　　C. 25　　　D. 27.5

㉖　If 1 cm = 0.39 inch, how many inches are there in 100 cm?

    A. 3.9　　　B. 39　　　C. 390　　　D. 3900

㉗ Mandy's mother buys her 2 new T-shirts at $9.50 each, 1 pair of jeans at $29.95 and 1 pair of sandals at $19.95. How much does Mandy's mother pay to the nearest dollar?

| A. $60 | B. $70 | C. $68 | D. $69 |

㉘ In August, Toronto's highest temperature is 35.5°C and the lowest temperature is 16.2°C. What is the difference between these temperatures?

| A. 51.7 °C | B. 19.3 °C | C. 26 °C | D. 29 °C |

㉙ The product of 1.6 and 2 is

| A. 3.6 | B. 0.8 | C. 3.2 | D. 1.4 |

㉚ When 1.2 is divided by 4, the quotient is

| A. 0.3 | B. 3.0 | C. 4.8 | D. 5.6 |

㉛ To calculate the average of 2 numbers is to add them up and then divide the sum by 2. The average of 13 and 10.2 is

| A. 23.2 | B. 11.6 | C. 1.6 | D. 3.2 |

㉜ When you divide a number by 10, the result is the same as multiplying the number by

| A. 10 | B. 0.1 | C. 0.01 | D. 100 |

㉝ When you multiply a number by 100, you move the decimal point

| A. 3 places to the right | B. 3 places to the left |
| C. 2 places to the right | D. 2 places to the left |

㉞ Which of the following statements is correct?

| A. $5 \div 2 = 0.5 \div 20$ | B. $5 \div 2 = 2 \div 5$ |
| C. $5 \div 2 = 50 \div 20$ | D. $5 \div 2 = 50 \div 0.2$ |

Ken's dog likes to run around in the backyard. Answer the questions using the measurements given in the diagram.

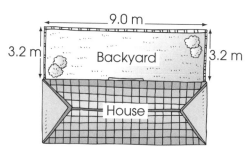

---

35 How much fencing is needed to enclose the backyard on 3 sides?

_____ m fencing is needed.

36 The fencing costs $20 per m. What is the total cost of the fencing?

37 What is the perimeter of the backyard?

38 What is the area of the backyard?

39 If both the width and the length of the backyard are doubled, what effect would this have on the perimeter and the area of the backyard?

a. perimeter

b. area

Introducing Fractions

1. Write a fraction for the shaded area in each diagram.

   a.  $\dfrac{1}{3}$

   b. $\dfrac{1}{4}$

   c. $\dfrac{3}{6} = \dfrac{1}{2}$

2. Write the fraction in its lowest terms.

   $$\dfrac{10}{15} = \dfrac{10 \div 5}{15 \div 5} = \dfrac{2}{3}$$

3. Label each of the divisions on the number line below. Write the fractions in lowest terms.

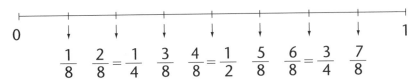

$\dfrac{1}{8}$ $\dfrac{2}{8} = \dfrac{1}{4}$ $\dfrac{3}{8}$ $\dfrac{4}{8} = \dfrac{1}{2}$ $\dfrac{5}{8}$ $\dfrac{6}{8} = \dfrac{3}{4}$ $\dfrac{7}{8}$

Write the fractions represented on the number line below.

① _____   ② _____

③ _____   ④ _____

HINTS:

- A fraction represents a part of a whole or a part of a set.

  e.g.   3 slices of an 8-slice pizza
         $= \dfrac{3}{8}$ of the pizza

- To represent a fraction in lowest terms (or simplest form), divide both the numerator and denominator by the same number.

- A fraction in lowest terms means the only number that will divide into both the numerator and denominator is 1.

Write a fraction for each shaded part.

⑤ _____

⑥ _____

⑦ _____

⑧ 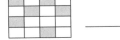 _____

⑨ _____

⑩ 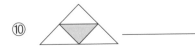 _____

Colour the diagrams to show each fraction.

⑪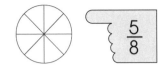

⑫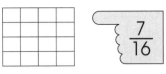

⑬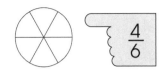

⑭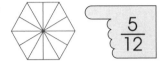

⑮

⑯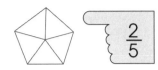

Place the following fractions on the number line below.

$$\frac{1}{10} \qquad \frac{2}{5} \qquad \frac{1}{2} \qquad \frac{9}{10} \qquad \frac{1}{20} \qquad \frac{4}{5}$$

⑰

Write a fraction for the grey shapes of each set.

⑱

⑲

⑳

_____   _____   _____

Colour the correct number of shapes grey to show each fraction.

㉑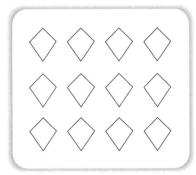

㉒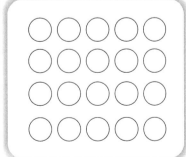

㉓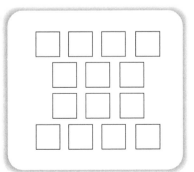

$$\frac{8}{12} \qquad\qquad\qquad \frac{11}{20} \qquad\qquad\qquad \frac{9}{14}$$

Colour and write the numbers.

㉔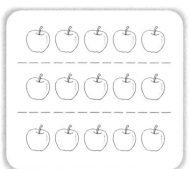

㉕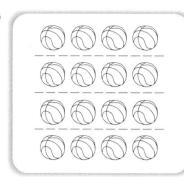

㉖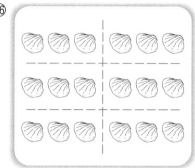

$\frac{1}{3}$ of 15 = _____

$\frac{3}{4}$ of 16 = _____

$\frac{2}{6}$ of 18 = _____

Fill in the boxes to express the following fractions in lowest terms.

㉗ $\frac{20}{30} = \frac{\boxed{}}{3}$

㉘ $\frac{5}{10} = \frac{1}{\boxed{}}$

㉙ $\frac{21}{28} = \frac{3}{\boxed{}}$

Write the following fractions in lowest terms.

㉚ $\frac{15}{20} =$ _____

㉛ $\frac{7}{21} =$ _____

㉜ $\frac{9}{18} =$ _____

㉝ $\frac{12}{18} =$ _____

㉞ $\frac{6}{16} =$ _____

㉟ $\frac{12}{15} =$ _____

Answer the following questions.

㊱ List any 3 fractions which lie between 0 and $\frac{1}{2}$. _____

㊲ What fraction of a dollar is represented by

    a. 7 nickels? _____

    b. 6 dimes? _____

㊳ Bill watches TV for 3 hours a day. What fraction of a day does he spend watching TV? _____

㊴ Margaret has 8 pairs of shoes. 6 pairs are black. What fraction of her shoes are not black? _____

㊵ Rick has finished reading 50 pages of a 250 page book. What fraction of the book has he read? _____

㊶ Pam is a rock climber. After she has climbed 30 m up a 45 m cliff, what fraction of the cliff must she climb to reach the top?

_____

㊷ 5 letters of the 26 letters in the alphabet are vowels. The others are consonants. What fraction of the alphabet do consonants make up?

_____

㊸ Tom worked 18 out of the 30 days in September. What fraction of the month did he work?

_____

㊹ Carol earns $7 per hour as a waitress. One weekend she worked for 10 hours and got $50 in tips. What fraction of her total earnings that day did her tips make up?

_____

㊺ Every day, Suzie sharpens her 16 cm long pencil and it loses 1 cm of its length. After 4 days, what fraction of its length remains?

_____

㊻ An ant crawls 50 cm along a 100 cm log the first day. The second day the ant crawls 25 cm and the third day it crawls 12 cm.

 a. What fraction of the log has it covered in three days? _____

 b. What fraction of the log remains to be covered till it reaches the end?

_____

Look for the pattern.

① What are the next 3 fractions?

$\dfrac{1}{2}$ $\dfrac{1}{4}$ $\dfrac{1}{8}$ _____ _____ _____ .

② If you continue the pattern, will you get to zero?

_____

Equivalent Fractions and Ordering of Fractions

1. Fill in the boxes to find the equivalent fractions of $\frac{2}{3}$.

$$\overset{\times 2 \quad\quad \times 5 \quad\quad \div 2}{\frac{2}{3} = \frac{\boxed{4}}{6} = \frac{\boxed{20}}{30} = \frac{\boxed{10}}{15}}$$

$$\underset{\times 2 \quad\quad \times 5 \quad\quad \div 2}{}$$

$$\frac{2}{3} = \frac{4}{6}$$

2. Order the following fractions from least to greatest.

$$\frac{2}{3} , \frac{5}{6} , \frac{7}{12} , \frac{1}{2}$$

$$\overset{\times 4}{\frac{2}{3} = \frac{8}{12}} \quad\quad \overset{\times 2}{\frac{5}{6} = \frac{10}{12}} \quad\quad \overset{\times 6}{\frac{1}{2} = \frac{6}{12}}$$

$$\therefore \quad \frac{1}{2} < \frac{7}{12} < \frac{2}{3} < \frac{5}{6}$$

HINTS:

- To find an equivalent fraction, multiply or divide the numerator and denominator by the same number.

- To compare the fractions, rewrite all fractions with the same denominator first and find their equivalent fractions. Then compare their numerators.

- Equivalent fractions are fractions that are equal in value.

Fill in the boxes to find the equivalent fractions.

① $\frac{1}{2} = \frac{\boxed{}}{50}$

② $\frac{5}{6} = \frac{\boxed{}}{30}$

③ $\frac{5}{7} = \frac{\boxed{}}{21}$

④ $\frac{3}{4} = \frac{\boxed{}}{100}$

⑤ $\frac{\boxed{}}{8} = \frac{14}{56}$

⑥ $\frac{11}{12} = \frac{\boxed{}}{84}$

Write each fraction in lowest terms.

⑦ $\frac{25}{30} = $ _____

⑧ $\frac{19}{38} = $ _____

⑨ $\frac{22}{121} = $ _____

⑩ $\frac{36}{84} = $ _____

⑪ $\frac{250}{1000} = $ _____

⑫ $\frac{32}{48} = $ _____

Circle the smaller fraction in each pair of fractions.

⑬ $\frac{3}{4}$ $\frac{7}{8}$ ⑭ $\frac{1}{3}$ $\frac{1}{2}$ ⑮ $\frac{1}{5}$ $\frac{1}{6}$

⑯ $\frac{5}{6}$ $\frac{2}{3}$ ⑰ $\frac{3}{7}$ $\frac{8}{21}$ ⑱ $\frac{4}{5}$ $\frac{11}{15}$

Order the fractions from least to greatest using < .

⑲ $\frac{3}{5}$ $\frac{4}{5}$ $\frac{1}{2}$ $\frac{1}{5}$ $\frac{1}{10}$ $\frac{7}{10}$ _____

⑳ $\frac{1}{3}$ $\frac{1}{4}$ $\frac{3}{4}$ $\frac{2}{3}$ $\frac{2}{4}$ _____

Write True (T) or False (F) for each statement.

㉑ $\frac{2}{3}$ < $\frac{4}{5}$ (   )   ㉒ $\frac{5}{9}$ < $\frac{1}{2}$ (   )

㉓ $\frac{21}{28}$ < $\frac{6}{7}$ (   )   ㉔ $\frac{24}{27}$ < $\frac{7}{9}$ (   )

Fill in the boxes.

㉕ $\frac{9}{15} = \frac{\Box}{5} = \frac{\Box}{20}$ ㉖ $\frac{9}{45} = \frac{1}{\Box} = \frac{\Box}{10}$

㉗ $\frac{14}{35} = \frac{\Box}{5} = \frac{\Box}{10}$ ㉘ $\frac{11}{\Box} = \frac{1}{5} = \frac{\Box}{20}$

Write 3 equivalent fractions for each of the following fractions.

㉙  $\frac{1}{8} = \Box = \Box = \Box$ ㉚ $\frac{2}{3} = \Box = \Box = \Box$

㉛  $\frac{1}{4} = \Box = \Box = \Box$ ㉜ $\frac{5}{7} = \Box = \Box = \Box$

Order each group of fractions from greatest to least using > .

㉝ $\dfrac{3}{4}$ $\dfrac{7}{8}$ $\dfrac{1}{2}$ $\dfrac{5}{8}$ $\dfrac{3}{16}$ $\dfrac{1}{4}$ $\dfrac{3}{8}$

_____

㉞ $\dfrac{2}{3}$ $\dfrac{1}{6}$ $\dfrac{7}{18}$ $\dfrac{1}{2}$ $\dfrac{5}{6}$ $\dfrac{13}{18}$ $\dfrac{1}{3}$

_____

Compare each pair of fractions and write > , < or = between them.

㉟ $\dfrac{5}{6}$ $\dfrac{7}{8}$ ㊱ $\dfrac{14}{18}$ $\dfrac{7}{9}$ ㊲ $\dfrac{11}{12}$ $\dfrac{9}{10}$

㊳ $\dfrac{2}{3}$ $\dfrac{11}{15}$ ㊴ $\dfrac{5}{16}$ $\dfrac{3}{8}$ ㊵ $\dfrac{15}{30}$ $\dfrac{7}{16}$

Write each fraction in lowest terms and order the fractions from least to greatest.

㊶ $\dfrac{15}{20}$ = _____   ㊷ $\dfrac{75}{125}$ = _____   ㊸ $\dfrac{45}{54}$ = _____

㊹ $\dfrac{200}{450}$ = _____   ㊺ $\dfrac{14}{18}$ = _____   ㊻ $\dfrac{150}{175}$ = _____

㊼ _____ < _____ < _____ < _____ < _____ < _____

Find the missing numbers.

㊽
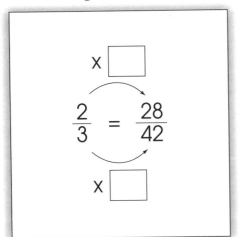

㊾
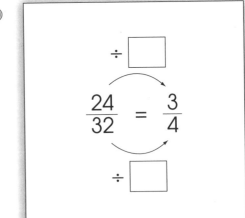

Answer the questions.

50. John gets 22 out of 25 on a test. What is his mark out of 100?

$$\frac{22}{25} = \frac{}{100}$$

His mark is _____.

51. Nadine gets 9 out of 12 in a quiz. Danielle gets 14 out of 18 in another quiz. Who has the better score?

_____

52. The table below shows the world population in 1994 and the projected value in 2025. (Use your calculator to calculate, if necessary.)

World Population (in millions)		
	1994	2025
Africa	682	1583
North Africa	373	498
Europe	512	542
World Total	5421	8474

a. What is the fraction of the world's population living in Africa in 1994? And in 2025?

In 1994 _____   In 2025 _____

b. Is this fraction increasing or decreasing from 1994 to 2025?   _____

c. What is the fraction of the world's population living in Europe in 1994? And in 2025?

In 1994 _____   In 2025 _____

d. Is this fraction increasing or decreasing from 1994 to 2025?   _____

Just for Fun

Look for the pattern. Write the next 3 terms.

1     $\frac{1}{4}$ $\frac{1}{9}$ _____ _____ _____

Adding Fractions with the Same Denominator

1. $\dfrac{1}{4} + \dfrac{3}{4} = \dfrac{1+3}{4} = \dfrac{4}{4} = \dfrac{4 \div 4}{4 \div 4} = 1$

add the numerators;
keep the denominator

reduce to lowest terms

HINTS:

- To add fractions with the same denominator, add the numerators and leave the denominator the same.

- Remember to reduce the sums to lowest terms.

- Reduce the fraction to 1 if its numerator and denominator are equal.

2. $\dfrac{1}{8} + \dfrac{5}{8} = \dfrac{1+5}{8} = \dfrac{6}{8} = \dfrac{3}{4}$

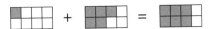

Find the sums mentally.

① $\dfrac{2}{3} + \dfrac{1}{3}$ = _____

② $\dfrac{1}{14} + \dfrac{13}{14}$ = _____

③ $\dfrac{1}{3} + \dfrac{1}{3}$ = _____

④ $\dfrac{1}{5} + \dfrac{1}{5}$ = _____

⑤ $\dfrac{1}{9} + \dfrac{4}{9}$ = _____

⑥ $\dfrac{1}{7} + \dfrac{3}{7}$ = _____

⑦ $\dfrac{3}{5} + \dfrac{1}{5}$ = _____

⑧ $\dfrac{1}{10} + \dfrac{9}{10}$ = _____

⑨ $\dfrac{5}{7} + \dfrac{2}{7}$ = _____

⑩ $\dfrac{1}{9} + \dfrac{7}{9}$ = _____

⑪ $\dfrac{1}{13} + \dfrac{10}{13}$ = _____

⑫ $\dfrac{5}{11} + \dfrac{3}{11}$ = _____

⑬ $\dfrac{2}{8} + \dfrac{5}{8}$ = _____

⑭ $\dfrac{6}{20} + \dfrac{7}{20}$ = _____

⑮ $\dfrac{5}{17} + \dfrac{4}{17}$ = _____

⑯ $\dfrac{6}{19} + \dfrac{3}{19}$ = _____

⑰ $\dfrac{4}{25} + \dfrac{17}{25}$ = _____

⑱ $\dfrac{5}{12} + \dfrac{5}{12}$ = _____

⑲ $\dfrac{4}{21} + \dfrac{13}{21}$ = _____

⑳ $\dfrac{7}{15} + \dfrac{1}{15}$ = _____

㉑ $\dfrac{1}{16} + \dfrac{5}{16}$ = _____

㉒ $\dfrac{1}{4} + \dfrac{1}{4}$ = _____

㉓ $\dfrac{5}{18} + \dfrac{7}{18}$ = _____

㉔ $\dfrac{11}{23} + \dfrac{11}{23}$ = _____

㉕ $\dfrac{1}{6} + \dfrac{3}{6}$ = _____

㉖ $\dfrac{14}{27} + \dfrac{11}{27}$ = _____

Add and reduce the answers to lowest terms. Show your work.

㉗ $\dfrac{6}{20} + \dfrac{7}{20}$ = _____

㉘ $\dfrac{4}{15} + \dfrac{8}{15}$ = _____

㉙ $\dfrac{2}{9} + \dfrac{1}{9}$ = _____

㉚ $\dfrac{11}{14} + \dfrac{1}{14}$ = _____

㉛ $\dfrac{5}{8} + \dfrac{1}{8}$ = _____

㉜ $\dfrac{3}{10} + \dfrac{3}{10}$ = _____

㉝ $\dfrac{3}{16} + \dfrac{5}{16}$ = _____

㉞ $\dfrac{1}{12} + \dfrac{5}{12}$ = _____

㉟ $\dfrac{1}{20} + \dfrac{3}{20}$ = _____

㊱ $\dfrac{1}{6} + \dfrac{1}{6}$ = _____

㊲ $\dfrac{3}{7} + \dfrac{1}{7}$ = _____

㊳ $\dfrac{1}{18} + \dfrac{2}{18}$ = _____

㊴ $\dfrac{1}{24} + \dfrac{5}{24}$ = _____

㊵ $\dfrac{5}{32} + \dfrac{3}{32}$ = _____

㊶ $\dfrac{2}{7} + \dfrac{3}{7} + \dfrac{2}{7}$ = _____

㊷ $\dfrac{2}{11} + \dfrac{2}{11} + \dfrac{3}{11} + \dfrac{4}{11}$ = _____

Complete each equation with a diagram. Then write each addition sentence using fractions. Give the sums in lowest terms.

㊸		+	⊘	=	$\dfrac{3}{8} + \dfrac{1}{8} =$ _____
㊹		+		=	_____
㊺		+		=	_____
㊻		+		=	_____
㊼		+		=	_____
㊽		+		=	_____

Fill in the boxes.

㊾ $\dfrac{3}{7} + \boxed{} = \dfrac{5}{7}$ $\qquad$ 50 $\dfrac{4}{11} + \boxed{} = \dfrac{5}{11}$

51 $\dfrac{1}{6} + \boxed{} = 1$ $\qquad$ 52 $\dfrac{1}{8} + \boxed{} = 1$

53 $\dfrac{1}{4} + \boxed{} = \dfrac{1}{2}$ $\qquad$ 54 $\dfrac{3}{8} + \boxed{} = \dfrac{1}{2}$

55 $\dfrac{8}{15} + \boxed{} = \dfrac{3}{5}$ $\qquad$ 56 $\dfrac{1}{10} + \boxed{} = \dfrac{1}{5}$

57 $\boxed{} + \dfrac{7}{20} = \dfrac{9}{10}$ $\qquad$ 58 $\boxed{} + \dfrac{7}{12} = 1$

59 $\boxed{} + \dfrac{9}{25} = \dfrac{4}{5}$ $\qquad$ 60 $\boxed{} + \dfrac{4}{9} = \dfrac{2}{3}$

Answer the questions. Show your work.

(61) Suzie has 3 dogs. They each eat $\frac{1}{4}$ of a tin of dog food each day. How much food do they eat among them each day?

They eat ________ tin of dog food.

(62) Bob, Carrie and Dan go out for pizza. They order 1 pizza. Bob and Carrie each eat $\frac{2}{6}$ of a pizza and Dan eats $\frac{1}{6}$ of a pizza.

a. How many pizzas do they eat among them?

b. Is there any pizza left?

(63) Janet needs 2 pieces of ribbon, one of $\frac{5}{8}$ m and the other of $\frac{1}{8}$ m.

a. How much ribbon does she need altogether?

b. If she buys 1 m of ribbon, will she have enough?

(64) Brenda spends $\frac{3}{10}$ of her weekly allowance on Monday and $\frac{1}{10}$ of her allowance on Tuesday.

a. What fraction of her allowance has she spent?

b. What fraction does she have left?

Find the missing fractions in the given magic square. The sum of each row, column and diagonal is the same.

$\frac{8}{15}$	$\frac{1}{15}$	$\frac{6}{15}$
	$\frac{5}{15}$	

Improper Fractions and Mixed Numbers

EXAMPLES

1. Change $\frac{13}{6}$ to a mixed number.

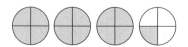

$$\frac{13}{6} = 2\frac{1}{6}$$

— quotient
— remainder
— original denominator

$$6\overline{)13} \quad 2 \text{ R }1$$
$$\underline{12}$$
$$1$$

2. Change $5\frac{3}{4}$ to an improper fraction.

$$5\frac{3}{4} = \frac{20}{4} + \frac{3}{4} = \frac{23}{4}$$

$$5 \times 4 = 20$$

3. Use a diagram to show that $3\frac{1}{4} = \frac{13}{4}$.

← Divide each circle into 4 equal parts. Shade 13 quarters.

4. Put $\frac{9}{2}$, $\frac{15}{4}$, $\frac{17}{5}$ in order from least to greatest.

$$\frac{9}{2} = 4\frac{1}{2} \qquad \frac{15}{4} = 3\frac{3}{4} \qquad \frac{17}{5} = 3\frac{2}{5}$$
$$= 4\frac{10}{20} \qquad\quad = 3\frac{15}{20} \qquad\quad = 3\frac{8}{20}$$

$$\therefore \; \frac{17}{5} < \frac{15}{4} < \frac{9}{2}$$

HINTS:

- Proper fraction: the numerator is smaller than the denominator
  e.g. $\frac{3}{7}$

- Improper fraction: the numerator is greater than or equal to the denominator
  e.g. $\frac{10}{7}$, $\frac{7}{7}$

- Mixed number: formed by a whole number and a proper fraction
  e.g. $1\frac{3}{7}$

- To convert an improper fraction to a mixed number, divide the numerator by the denominator. The quotient is the whole number part of the mixed number. The remainder is the new numerator. The denominator is unchanged.

- To convert a mixed number to an improper fraction, the denominator is unchanged. The new numerator is the sum of the old numerator and the product of the whole number and the denominator.

Complete the table.

	Improper Fraction	Mixed Number
①	$\frac{15}{7}$	
②		$3\frac{3}{8}$
③	$\frac{11}{3}$	
④		$11\frac{1}{4}$
⑤	$\frac{7}{5}$	

Write the fractions or mixed numbers on the right screens.

$$3\frac{3}{10} \quad \frac{9}{9} \quad \frac{4}{7} \quad \frac{5}{20} \quad \frac{25}{20} \quad \frac{7}{9} \quad 3\frac{1}{2} \quad 1\frac{5}{20} \quad \frac{15}{8} \quad \frac{11}{12} \quad \frac{16}{7} \quad 1\frac{2}{5}$$

⑥ Proper Fraction

_____ _____

_____ _____

⑦ Improper Fraction

_____ _____

_____ _____

⑧ Mixed Number

_____ _____

_____ _____

Write the mixed numbers represented by each group of the following diagrams. Then convert each to an improper fraction.

⑨

mixed number _____

improper fraction _____

⑩

mixed number _____

improper fraction _____

Place the improper fractions on the number line below.

$$\frac{3}{2} \quad \frac{15}{4} \quad \frac{17}{5} \quad \frac{5}{2} \quad \frac{7}{3} \quad \frac{6}{5} \quad \frac{23}{5}$$

⑪

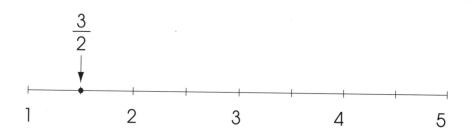

$$\frac{3}{2}$$

1   2   3   4   5

Write an improper fraction to represent each number on the number line below.

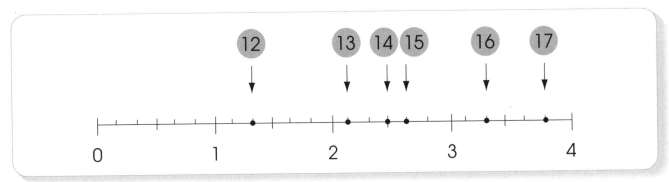

⑫ _____   ⑬ _____   ⑭ _____

⑮ _____   ⑯ _____   ⑰ _____

Order the fractions from greatest to least using > .

⑱ $\dfrac{5}{3}$ $\dfrac{7}{2}$ $\dfrac{9}{4}$ $\dfrac{7}{3}$ $\dfrac{15}{4}$ _____

⑲ $\dfrac{17}{2}$ $\dfrac{17}{5}$ $\dfrac{17}{6}$ $\dfrac{17}{3}$ $\dfrac{17}{4}$ _____

Circle the right numbers in each group.

⑳ The numbers between 3 and 4

$\dfrac{22}{3}$ $\dfrac{15}{7}$ $\dfrac{23}{6}$ $\dfrac{19}{6}$ $\dfrac{17}{4}$ $\dfrac{7}{2}$

㉑ The numbers between 8 and 9

$\dfrac{27}{4}$ $\dfrac{60}{7}$ $\dfrac{49}{6}$ $\dfrac{15}{2}$ $\dfrac{37}{5}$ $\dfrac{25}{3}$

Match the fractions and the mixed numbers.

㉒

$1\dfrac{1}{2}$ $4\dfrac{1}{2}$ $\dfrac{2}{3}$ $\dfrac{12}{9}$ $1\dfrac{3}{8}$ $1\dfrac{2}{5}$ $\dfrac{36}{5}$

$\dfrac{9}{2}$ $\dfrac{12}{18}$ $\dfrac{36}{24}$ $\dfrac{7}{5}$ $7\dfrac{1}{5}$ $1\dfrac{1}{3}$ $\dfrac{11}{8}$

Answer the questions. Show your work. Drawing diagrams may be helpful.

㉓　5 friends each drink $\frac{1}{2}$ L of juice. How much juice do they drink? Write your answer

　　a.　as a mixed number.　　　　　　　　　　　　　　　　 _____

　　b.　as an improper fraction.　　　　　　　　　　　　　　 _____

㉔　Joanne has $2\frac{1}{4}$ dollars in her pocket. The coins are all quarters. How many quarters does she have?

　　　　　　　　　　　　　　　　　　　　　　　　　 _____ quarters

㉕　Each worker paves $\frac{1}{5}$ of a driveway per day. How many driveways do 8 workers pave per day?

　　　　　　　　　　　　　　　　　　　　　　　　　 _____ driveways

㉖　A group of students eat $4\frac{1}{2}$ pizzas among them. If they eat $\frac{1}{2}$ pizza each, how many students are there?

　　　　　　　　　　　　　　　　　　　　　　　　　 _____ students

㉗　Candy says that $\frac{15}{4}$ is greater than $\frac{13}{3}$ since 15 > 13 and 4 > 3. Is this statement true or false? Explain.

How many sixteenths are there in three and a half?

There are _____ sixteenths.

Adding Improper Fractions and Mixed Numbers

1. $\dfrac{13}{7} + \dfrac{1}{7} = \dfrac{13 + 1}{7}$ ← add the numerators; keep the denominator

$= \dfrac{14}{7}$

$= 2$ ← reduce to lowest terms

2. $1\dfrac{1}{4} + 2\dfrac{1}{4} = \dfrac{5}{4} + \dfrac{9}{4}$ ← change mixed number to improper fraction

$= \dfrac{14}{4}$

$= 3\dfrac{1}{2}$ ← change back to mixed number

3. $1\dfrac{1}{4} + 2\dfrac{1}{4} = 1 + \dfrac{1}{4} + 2 + \dfrac{1}{4}$ ← split the mixed numbers into whole numbers and fractions

$= 3 + \dfrac{1 + 1}{4}$ ← add the whole numbers and fractions separately

$= 3\dfrac{2}{4}$

$= 3\dfrac{1}{2}$ ← reduce to lowest terms

HINTS:

- Adding mixed numbers:

  change the mixed numbers to improper fractions and add the fractions;

  or

  add the whole numbers and fractions separately.

- Remember to reduce the sums to lowest terms.

- If the sum is an improper fraction, change back to a mixed number.

Find the sums mentally. All the answers are whole numbers.

① $\quad 1\dfrac{1}{2} + \dfrac{1}{2} = \underline{\hspace{1.5cm}}$

② $\quad 2\dfrac{1}{3} + \dfrac{2}{3} = \underline{\hspace{1.5cm}}$

③ $\quad 4\dfrac{1}{4} + \dfrac{3}{4} = \underline{\hspace{1.5cm}}$ ④ $\quad \dfrac{8}{3} + \dfrac{1}{3} = \underline{\hspace{1.5cm}}$ ⑤ $\quad \dfrac{11}{2} + \dfrac{3}{2} = \underline{\hspace{1.5cm}}$

⑥ $\quad \dfrac{11}{5} + \dfrac{4}{5} = \underline{\hspace{1.5cm}}$ ⑦ $\quad 5\dfrac{3}{5} + \dfrac{2}{5} = \underline{\hspace{1.5cm}}$ ⑧ $\quad \dfrac{17}{3} + \dfrac{4}{3} = \underline{\hspace{1.5cm}}$

⑨ $\quad \dfrac{2}{9} + 2\dfrac{7}{9} = \underline{\hspace{1.5cm}}$ ⑩ $\quad \dfrac{11}{6} + \dfrac{1}{6} = \underline{\hspace{1.5cm}}$ ⑪ $\quad 1\dfrac{2}{7} + \dfrac{5}{7} = \underline{\hspace{1.5cm}}$

⑫ $\quad \dfrac{5}{8} + 2\dfrac{3}{8} = \underline{\hspace{1.5cm}}$ ⑬ $\quad \dfrac{3}{10} + 3\dfrac{7}{10} = \underline{\hspace{1.5cm}}$ ⑭ $\quad \dfrac{13}{11} + \dfrac{9}{11} = \underline{\hspace{1.5cm}}$

Find the sums. Show your work. Write the answers in lowest terms as mixed numbers.

⑮ $2\frac{1}{8} + \frac{1}{8}$ = _____

⑯ $4\frac{2}{5} + 2\frac{1}{5}$ = _____

⑰ $3\frac{1}{5} + \frac{1}{5}$ = _____

⑱ $5\frac{1}{4} + \frac{1}{4}$ = _____

⑲ $\frac{11}{5} + \frac{6}{5}$ = _____

⑳ $1\frac{3}{4} + 1\frac{3}{4}$ = _____

㉑ $\frac{3}{8} + \frac{9}{8}$ = _____

㉒ $2\frac{2}{3} + 1\frac{2}{3}$ = _____

㉓ $\frac{3}{10} + \frac{13}{10}$ = _____

㉔ $2\frac{7}{16} + \frac{7}{16}$ = _____

㉕ $2\frac{7}{8} + \frac{3}{8}$ = _____

㉖ $\frac{3}{10} + \frac{17}{10}$ = _____

㉗ $1\frac{3}{8} + 3\frac{3}{8}$ = _____

㉘ $\frac{13}{6} + \frac{1}{6}$ = _____

㉙ $4\frac{1}{5} + 3\frac{2}{5} + 1\frac{4}{5}$ = _____

㉚ $\frac{5}{6} + 1\frac{1}{6} + 4$ = _____

Fill in the boxes.

③① $1\frac{1}{4} + \boxed{} = 2$

③② $3\frac{3}{8} + \boxed{} = 4$

③③ $\boxed{} + 1\frac{1}{5} = 3$

③④ $\boxed{} + 3\frac{1}{2} = 5$

③⑤ $\frac{3}{2} + \boxed{} = 2$

③⑥ $\frac{7}{5} + \boxed{} = 2$

③⑦ $5\frac{1}{3} + \boxed{} = 6$

③⑧ $\frac{11}{6} + \boxed{} = 3$

③⑨ $\boxed{} + \frac{4}{5} = 4$

④⓪ $\boxed{} + 4\frac{1}{4} = 5$

Write True (T) or False (F) for each of the following statements.

④① $\frac{2}{3} + \frac{2}{3} > 1$ ( )

④② $1\frac{3}{4} + \frac{1}{2} > 2$ ( )

④③ $\frac{1}{3} + \frac{1}{3} > \frac{5}{6}$ ( )

④④ $2\frac{1}{2} < 2\frac{4}{7}$ ( )

④⑤ $1\frac{3}{8} + \frac{3}{4} > 2$ ( )

④⑥ $1\frac{1}{3} > 1\frac{4}{11}$ ( )

④⑦ $1\frac{2}{5} = \frac{7}{5}$ ( )

④⑧ $3\frac{1}{3} > 3\frac{1}{2}$ ( )

Answer only the questions that have a sum greater than 3.

④⑨ $2\frac{2}{3} + \frac{2}{3} =$ _____

⑤⓪ $2\frac{1}{3} + \frac{1}{3} =$ _____

⑤① $\frac{15}{7} + \frac{5}{7} =$ _____

⑤② $1\frac{5}{8} + 1\frac{7}{8} =$ _____

⑤③ $\frac{9}{4} + \frac{5}{4} =$ _____

⑤④ $\frac{4}{5} + \frac{12}{5} =$ _____

⑤⑤ $\frac{5}{6} + 1\frac{5}{6} =$ _____

⑤⑥ $1\frac{7}{9} + 1\frac{7}{9} =$ _____

Answer the questions. Show your work.

57. Ann has 3 cats. Shadow eats $1\frac{1}{4}$ cans of food per week. Rocky eats $2\frac{1}{4}$ cans and Peppy eats $1\frac{3}{4}$ cans. How many cans of food do they eat among them per week?

58. Shares in Riverview International were sold for $45\frac{3}{8}$ ¢ per share. They increase in value by $2\frac{1}{8}$ ¢. What is the new selling price?

59. Janet is sewing 2 dresses. One needs $3\frac{1}{8}$ m of fabric and the other needs $4\frac{3}{4}$ m.

   a. How much fabric must she buy?

   b. Would 8 m be enough?

60. Peggy keeps a record of her weekly TV watching in the chart below.

Day	Sun.	Mon.	Tue.	Wed.	Thu.	Fri.	Sat.
Time (hours)	$1\frac{1}{4}$	$1\frac{1}{4}$	$\frac{3}{4}$	$1\frac{1}{4}$	2	$1\frac{3}{4}$	$2\frac{3}{4}$

How much TV did she watch during the week?

Look for the pattern. Fill in the missing number.

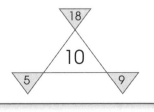

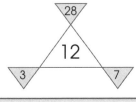

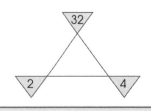

Subtracting Fractions with the Same Denominator

1. $\dfrac{3}{8} - \dfrac{1}{8} = \dfrac{3-1}{8}$ ←—— subtract the numerators; keep the denominator

   $= \dfrac{2}{8}$

   $= \dfrac{1}{4}$ ←—— reduce to lowest terms

2. $\dfrac{6}{10} - \dfrac{1}{10} = \dfrac{6-1}{10} = \dfrac{5}{10} = \dfrac{1}{2}$

HINTS:

- To subtract fractions with the same denominator, subtract the numerators and leave the denominator the same.

- Remember to reduce the difference to lowest terms.

- If the difference is an improper fraction, change back to a mixed number.

Find the differences mentally.

① $\dfrac{3}{7} - \dfrac{1}{7} = \underline{\hspace{2cm}}$

② $\dfrac{11}{12} - \dfrac{10}{12} = \underline{\hspace{2cm}}$

③ $\dfrac{8}{9} - \dfrac{1}{9} = \underline{\hspace{2cm}}$

④ $\dfrac{9}{11} - \dfrac{7}{11} = \underline{\hspace{2cm}}$

⑤ $\dfrac{3}{7} - \dfrac{1}{7} = \underline{\hspace{2cm}}$

⑥ $\dfrac{5}{10} - \dfrac{4}{10} = \underline{\hspace{2cm}}$

⑦ $\dfrac{16}{17} - \dfrac{13}{17} = \underline{\hspace{2cm}}$

⑧ $\dfrac{5}{12} - \dfrac{5}{12} = \underline{\hspace{2cm}}$

⑨ $\dfrac{8}{15} - \dfrac{7}{15} = \underline{\hspace{2cm}}$

⑩ $\dfrac{5}{8} - \dfrac{3}{8} = \underline{\hspace{2cm}}$

⑪ $\dfrac{11}{13} - \dfrac{9}{13} = \underline{\hspace{2cm}}$

⑫ $\dfrac{13}{14} - \dfrac{9}{14} = \underline{\hspace{2cm}}$

Complete each equation with a diagram.

⑬
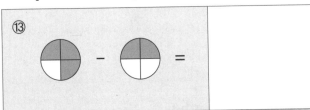

⑭
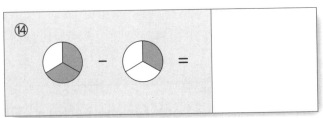

⑮
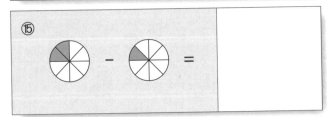

⑯
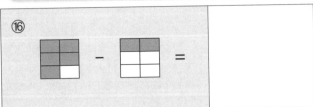

Subtract and reduce the answers to lowest terms. Show your work.

⑰ $\dfrac{9}{10} - \dfrac{4}{10} =$ _____

⑱ $\dfrac{5}{8} - \dfrac{1}{8} =$ _____

⑲ $\dfrac{4}{9} - \dfrac{1}{9} =$ _____

⑳ $\dfrac{7}{12} - \dfrac{4}{12} =$ _____

㉑ $\dfrac{5}{6} - \dfrac{1}{6} =$ _____

㉒ $\dfrac{13}{16} - \dfrac{1}{16} =$ _____

㉓ $\dfrac{3}{4} - \dfrac{1}{4} =$ _____

㉔ $\dfrac{10}{14} - \dfrac{2}{14} =$ _____

㉕ $\dfrac{7}{9} - \dfrac{1}{9} =$ _____

㉖ $\dfrac{3}{8} - \dfrac{1}{8} =$ _____

㉗ $\dfrac{17}{20} - \dfrac{2}{20} =$ _____

㉘ $\dfrac{42}{50} - \dfrac{12}{50} =$ _____

㉙ $\dfrac{16}{24} - \dfrac{8}{24} =$ _____

㉚ $\dfrac{13}{25} - \dfrac{3}{25} =$ _____

㉛ $\dfrac{19}{26} - \dfrac{6}{26} =$ _____

㉜ $\dfrac{6}{12} - \dfrac{1}{12} - \dfrac{2}{12} =$ _____

Fill in the missing number in each box.

㉝ $\frac{1}{4} + \square = 1$

㉞ $\square + \frac{4}{7} = \frac{5}{7}$

㉟ $\frac{5}{7} - \square = \frac{1}{7}$

㊱ $\frac{3}{4} - \square = \frac{1}{4}$

㊲ $\square + \frac{1}{2} = \frac{3}{4}$

㊳ $\square - \frac{1}{9} = \frac{7}{9}$

㊴ $\square + \frac{4}{5} = 1$

㊵ $\frac{5}{9} + \square = 1$

㊶ $\frac{5}{6} - \square = \frac{2}{3}$

㊷ $\square - \frac{1}{4} = \frac{1}{2}$

㊸ $\frac{1}{9} + \square = \frac{7}{9}$

㊹ $\frac{3}{9} + \square = \frac{5}{9}$

㊺ $\square - \frac{1}{3} = \frac{1}{3}$

㊻ $\frac{1}{5} + \square = \frac{3}{5}$

㊼ $\square - \frac{1}{10} = \frac{1}{5}$

㊽ $\frac{3}{11} + \square = \frac{8}{11}$

㊾ $\frac{3}{10} + \frac{1}{10} = \square$

㊿ $\frac{5}{8} - \square = \frac{1}{2}$

Find the answers.

(51) $\frac{1}{7} + \frac{5}{7} - \frac{4}{7} = \frac{1 + 5 - 4}{7} =$ ________

(52) $\frac{4}{12} + \frac{7}{12} - \frac{5}{12} =$ ________ $=$ ________

(53) $\frac{11}{18} - \frac{7}{18} + \frac{1}{18} =$ ________ $=$ ________

Answer the questions. Show your work.

54 Ron read $\frac{5}{8}$ of his book on Monday and $\frac{3}{8}$ on Tuesday. How much did he read on Monday than on Tuesday?

He read _____ more of his book on Monday.

55 Ben takes $\frac{3}{4}$ hour to do his Math homework but Carla only takes $\frac{1}{4}$ hour. How much longer does Ben take?

56 Carol takes $\frac{5}{6}$ hour to walk to school. Dave takes $\frac{1}{6}$ hour for the same walk. How much less time does Dave take?

57 Paula takes 40 minutes to wash her car.

    a. What fraction of the job will she have done after 10 minutes?

    b. What fraction of the job still remains?

58 Bob buys 10 plants for his garden. 2 are violet and 4 are red.

    a. What fraction of the plants are violet? What fraction are red?

    b. What fraction of the plants are neither red nor violet?

Fill in the missing numbers.

$$
\begin{array}{r}
\boxed{}\ 7\ 4\ 5\ 6\ 1 \\
-\qquad 8\ \boxed{}\ 1\ \boxed{}\ 3 \\
\hline
7\ \boxed{}\ 7\ \boxed{}\ 7\ \boxed{}
\end{array}
$$

Subtracting Improper Fractions and Mixed Numbers

1. $1 - \dfrac{3}{5}$ $= \dfrac{5}{5} - \dfrac{3}{5}$ ← $\dfrac{5}{5} = 1$

           $= \dfrac{2}{5}$

2. $2\dfrac{4}{5} - 1\dfrac{3}{5} = \dfrac{14}{5} - \dfrac{8}{5}$ ← change mixed numbers to improper fractions

           $= \dfrac{14 - 8}{5}$ ← subtract the numerators; keep the denominator

           $= \dfrac{6}{5}$

           $= 1\dfrac{1}{5}$ ← change back to mixed number

           or

3. $2\dfrac{4}{5} - 1\dfrac{3}{5} = 2 + \dfrac{4}{5} - 1 - \dfrac{3}{5}$ ← split the mixed numbers

           $= 2 - 1 + \dfrac{4 - 3}{5}$ ← subtract the whole numbers and fractions separately

           $= 1\dfrac{1}{5}$

HINTS:

- Subtracting mixed numbers:

  Change mixed numbers to improper fractions and subtract the fractions; or

  subtract the whole numbers and fractions separately.

- Remember to reduce the difference to lowest terms.

- If the difference is an improper fraction, change back to a mixed number.

Find the differences mentally.

① $2\dfrac{4}{7} - \dfrac{3}{7}$ = _____

② $2\dfrac{3}{5} - \dfrac{1}{5}$ = _____

③ $\dfrac{11}{9} - \dfrac{4}{9}$ = _____

④ $1\dfrac{7}{8} - 1\dfrac{6}{8}$ = _____

⑤ $\dfrac{21}{4} - \dfrac{18}{4}$ = _____

⑥ $5\dfrac{3}{4} - 5$ = _____

⑦ $\dfrac{3}{2} - \dfrac{3}{2}$ = _____

⑧ $12\dfrac{3}{9} - 12\dfrac{1}{9}$ = _____

⑨ $5\dfrac{1}{3} - 2\dfrac{1}{3}$ = _____

⑩ $1\dfrac{4}{9} - 1\dfrac{3}{9}$ = _____

⑪ $8\dfrac{7}{13} - 8\dfrac{4}{13}$ = _____

⑫ $\dfrac{13}{10} - \dfrac{3}{10}$ = _____

⑬ $10\dfrac{7}{8} - 10$ = _____

⑭ $\dfrac{10}{3} - \dfrac{8}{3}$ = _____

⑮ $3\dfrac{5}{6} - 3\dfrac{1}{6}$ = _____

⑯ $9\dfrac{7}{8} - 4\dfrac{7}{8}$ = _____

Find the differences. Show your work. Write the answers in lowest terms.

⑰ $1\dfrac{1}{2} - \dfrac{3}{2} =$ _____

⑱ $2\dfrac{3}{4} - \dfrac{1}{4} =$ _____

⑲ $\dfrac{6}{5} - \dfrac{1}{5} =$ _____

⑳ $\dfrac{9}{4} - \dfrac{3}{4} =$ _____

㉑ $5\dfrac{1}{4} - 4\dfrac{3}{4} =$ _____

㉒ $3\dfrac{1}{8} - 2\dfrac{7}{8} =$ _____

㉓ $\dfrac{11}{4} - \dfrac{3}{4} =$ _____

㉔ $\dfrac{12}{10} - \dfrac{8}{10} =$ _____

㉕ $2\dfrac{1}{6} - 1\dfrac{5}{6} =$ _____

㉖ $\dfrac{20}{9} - \dfrac{11}{9} =$ _____

㉗ $2\dfrac{3}{8} - \dfrac{9}{8} =$ _____

㉘ $1\dfrac{1}{11} - \dfrac{12}{11} =$ _____

㉙ $\dfrac{21}{10} - 1\dfrac{1}{10} =$ _____

㉚ $\dfrac{21}{3} - 5\dfrac{1}{3} =$ _____

㉛ $5\dfrac{3}{4} - 2\dfrac{1}{4} - \dfrac{2}{4} =$ _____

㉜ $9 - 6\dfrac{1}{5} - 1\dfrac{3}{5} =$ _____

Fill in the missing number in each box.

㉝ $1\dfrac{1}{4} - \dfrac{3}{4} = \boxed{}$

㉞ $\dfrac{13}{5} - \boxed{} = \dfrac{9}{5}$

㉟ $\dfrac{5}{3} + \boxed{} = 2$

㊱ $\boxed{} - 1\dfrac{3}{4} = 3\dfrac{1}{4}$

㊲ $\boxed{} - \dfrac{1}{4} = 1\dfrac{1}{4}$

㊳ $\boxed{} + 2\dfrac{1}{4} = 3$

㊴ $\boxed{} - 3\dfrac{3}{8} = \dfrac{5}{8}$

㊵ $\dfrac{5}{3} - \boxed{} = 0$

㊶ $\dfrac{5}{4} + \boxed{} = 2$

㊷ $\boxed{} + \dfrac{4}{7} = 3$

㊸ $\dfrac{7}{5} - \boxed{} = 1$

㊹ $\dfrac{1}{2} + \boxed{} = 4$

㊺ $2 - \boxed{} = 1\dfrac{1}{3}$

㊻ $\boxed{} - \dfrac{1}{9} = \dfrac{8}{9}$

㊼ $\boxed{} + \dfrac{3}{4} = 1\dfrac{1}{4}$

㊽ $\boxed{} + \dfrac{6}{5} = 2$

Find the answers.

㊾ $3\dfrac{4}{6} + 4\dfrac{1}{6} - 2\dfrac{2}{6} = \rule{4cm}{0.4pt} = \rule{2cm}{0.4pt}$

㊿ $9 - 3\dfrac{1}{8} + 1\dfrac{2}{8} = \rule{4cm}{0.4pt} = \rule{2cm}{0.4pt}$

51 $4\dfrac{1}{6} - 3\dfrac{3}{6} + 1\dfrac{4}{6} = \rule{4cm}{0.4pt} = \rule{2cm}{0.4pt}$

52 $3\dfrac{2}{7} + 2\dfrac{4}{7} - 1\dfrac{5}{7} = \rule{4cm}{0.4pt} = \rule{2cm}{0.4pt}$

Answer the questions. Show your work. Write the fractions in lowest terms.

(53) On Monday, Jonathan watched TV for $2\frac{3}{4}$ hours and Pat watched TV for $3\frac{1}{4}$ hours. How much longer did Pat spend watching TV?

(54) On Monday, Ron ran $8\frac{3}{8}$ km and on Wednesday he ran $6\frac{5}{8}$ km. How much farther did he run on Monday?

(55) ABC shares sell for $3\frac{1}{5}$ dollars each and BFI share sell for $2\frac{4}{5}$ dollars each. What is the difference between the share prices?

(56) The perimeter of the triangle is 1 m. What is the length of the third side?

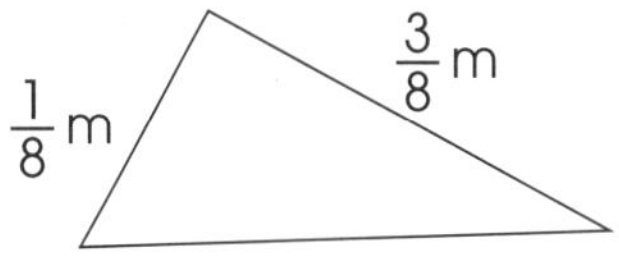

(57) The dimensions of a framed picture are $15\frac{1}{4}$ cm by $10\frac{1}{2}$ cm. The frame is $1\frac{1}{2}$ cm wide. What are the dimensions of the unframed part of the picture?

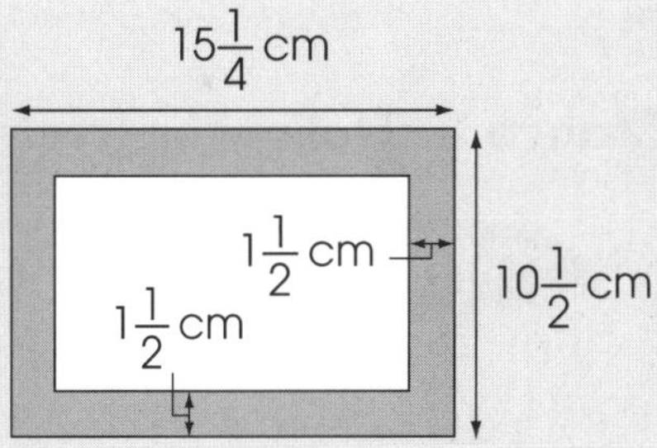

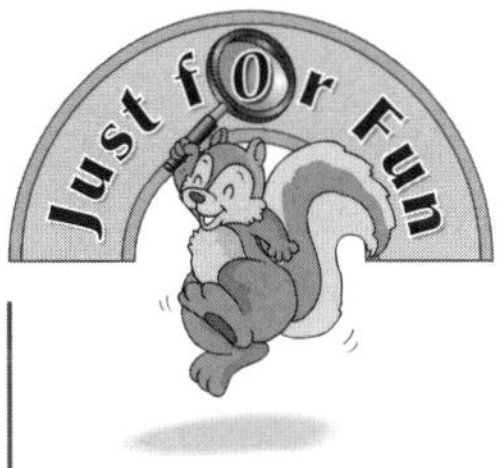

7 people eat $\frac{1}{4}$ of a pizza each. If they buy 2 pizzas, how much pizza is left?

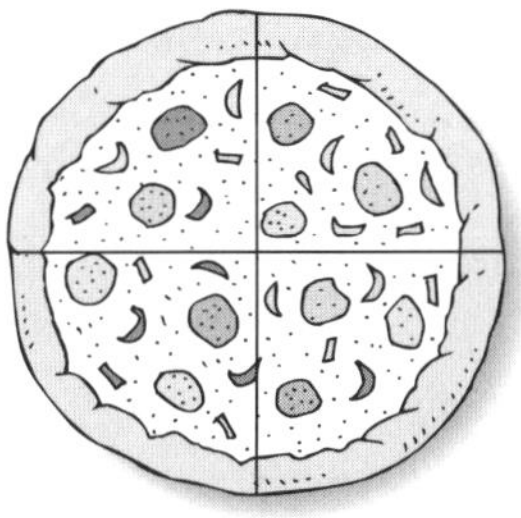

______________ pizza is left.

Relating Decimals and Fractions

1. Convert 0.7 and 0.55 to fractions.

$$0.7 = \frac{7}{10}$$ ← put 1 zero in the denominator since 0.7 has 1 decimal place

$$0.55 = \frac{55}{100} = \frac{11}{20}$$ ← reduce the fraction to lowest terms

put 2 zeros in the denominator since 0.55 has 2 decimal places

2. Convert $\frac{1}{4}$ and $2\frac{1}{5}$ to decimals

$$\frac{1}{4} = 0.25$$

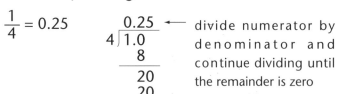

← divide numerator by denominator and continue dividing until the remainder is zero

$$2\frac{1}{5} = 2 + \frac{1}{5} = 2 + 0.2 = 2.2$$

change the fraction part to decimal

HINTS:

- Change decimals to fractions:

  Write the decimal part as numerator with a denominator of 10, 100, 1000 etc.

  e.g. $0.07 = \frac{7}{100}$ ← number of zeros in the denominator equals the number of decimal places

  Remember to reduce the fractions to lowest terms.

- Change fractions to decimals:

  Find the equivalent fraction with a denominator of 10, 100, 1000 etc, and then write the fraction as a decimal number.

  e.g. $\frac{1}{4} = \frac{1 \times 25}{4 \times 25} = \frac{25}{100} = 0.25$ or

  divide the numerator by the denominator; continue dividing until the remainder is zero or there are enough decimal places.

  e.g. $\frac{2}{3} = 0.67$ ← round to the nearest hundredth

Change the following fractions to decimals.

Fraction	Decimal
① $\frac{1}{10}$	_____
② $\frac{7}{10}$	_____
③ $\frac{3}{100}$	_____
④ $\frac{49}{100}$	_____
⑤ $\frac{9}{100}$	_____
⑥ $\frac{73}{100}$	_____

Change the following decimals to fractions.

Decimal	Fraction
⑦ 0.3	_____
⑨ 0.9	_____
⑪ 0.09	_____
⑬ 0.31	_____
⑮ 0.47	_____

Decimal	Fraction
⑧ 0.7	_____
⑩ 0.01	_____
⑫ 0.07	_____
⑭ 0.19	_____
⑯ 0.03	_____

Use division to convert each of the following fractions to decimals.

Fraction	Decimal
⑰ $\frac{1}{2}$	_____
⑲ $\frac{3}{4}$	_____
㉑ $\frac{1}{8}$	_____
㉓ $\frac{3}{8}$	_____

Fraction	Decimal
⑱ $\frac{1}{5}$	_____
⑳ $\frac{3}{5}$	_____
㉒ $\frac{5}{8}$	_____
㉔ $\frac{4}{5}$	_____

Convert the following fractions to decimals. Round the answers to the nearest hundredth if necessary.

㉕ $1\frac{5}{8}$ = _____   ㉖ $3\frac{4}{7}$ = _____   ㉗ $12\frac{4}{5}$ = _____

㉘ $2\frac{3}{8}$ = _____   ㉙ $3\frac{5}{6}$ = _____   ㉚ $5\frac{4}{9}$ = _____

㉛ $1\frac{2}{3}$ = _____   ㉜ $2\frac{3}{5}$ = _____   ㉝ $4\frac{1}{4}$ = _____

㉞ $10\frac{2}{5}$ = _____   ㉟ $8\frac{6}{7}$ = _____   ㊱ $6\frac{7}{10}$ = _____

Change the decimals to fractions. Give your answers in lowest terms.

③⑦ $0.65 = \dfrac{65}{100} = $ _____

③⑧ $0.75 = $ _____ $= $ _____

③⑨ $0.05 = $ _____ $= $ _____

④⓪ $0.12 = $ _____ $= $ _____

④① $0.45 = $ _____ $= $ _____

④② $0.36 = $ _____ $= $ _____

④③ $1.45 = $ _____ $= $ _____

④④ $6.55 = $ _____ $= $ _____

④⑤ $2.8 = $ _____ $= $ _____

④⑥ $2.25 = $ _____ $= $ _____

How many cents are there in each of the following fractions of a dollar?

④⑦ $\$\dfrac{1}{4} = $ _____ ¢

④⑧ $\$\dfrac{3}{4} = $ _____ ¢

④⑨ $\$\dfrac{2}{5} = $ _____ ¢

⑤⓪ $\$\dfrac{3}{5} = $ _____ ¢

⑤① $\$\dfrac{7}{10} = $ _____ ¢

⑤② $\$\dfrac{9}{10} = $ _____ ¢

Circle the larger number in each pair.

⑤③ $0.65 \quad \dfrac{1}{2}$

⑤④ $\dfrac{4}{5} \quad 0.9$

⑤⑤ $1.3 \quad 1\dfrac{2}{5}$

⑤⑥ $\dfrac{2}{3} \quad 0.62$

⑤⑦ $4.26 \quad 4\dfrac{1}{4}$

⑤⑧ $0.57 \quad \dfrac{8}{15}$

⑤⑨ $3.69 \quad 3\dfrac{3}{5}$

⑥⓪ $8.38 \quad 8\dfrac{1}{3}$

⑥① $6\dfrac{3}{8} \quad 6.37$

Arrange the following numbers in order from least to greatest.

⑥② $1\dfrac{7}{8} \quad 1.54 \quad 1\dfrac{8}{9}$ _____ < _____ < _____

⑥③ $2.68 \quad 2\dfrac{3}{5} \quad 2\dfrac{4}{7}$ _____ < _____ < _____

⑥④ $5\dfrac{9}{10} \quad 5\dfrac{4}{5} \quad 5.83$ _____ < _____ < _____

Complete the table. Then list the fractions in order from least to greatest.

Fraction	$\frac{1}{8}$	$\frac{1}{4}$	$\frac{3}{4}$	$\frac{3}{8}$	$\frac{7}{8}$	$\frac{1}{5}$	$\frac{7}{10}$
⑥⑤ Decimal							

⑥⑥ _____ < _____ < _____ < _____ < _____ < _____ < _____

Answer the questions.

⑥⑦ Canada produces about 0.24 of the world's supply of nickel ore. Express this as a fraction in lowest terms. _____

⑥⑧ Paul climbs 100 steps up a 160-step tower.

    a. What fraction of the tower has he climbed? _____

    b. Express your answer as a decimal. _____

⑥⑨ $\frac{2}{5}$ of the cost of a litre of gas is tax.

    a. Express this fraction as a decimal. _____

    b. If gas costs 75¢ a litre, how much is the tax? _____

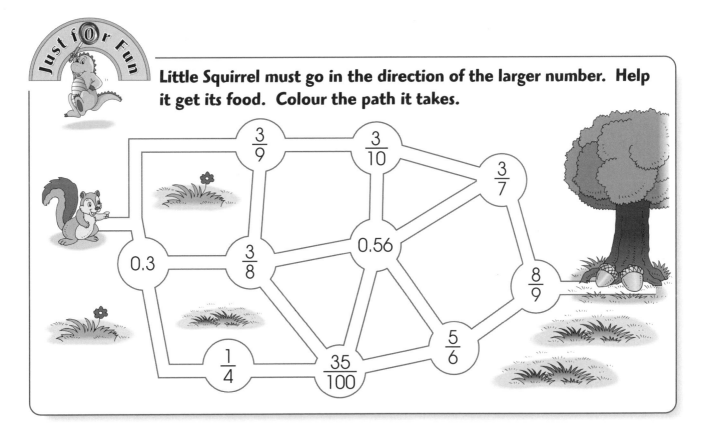

Just f0r Fun

Little Squirrel must go in the direction of the larger number. Help it get its food. Colour the path it takes.

Final Review

Circle the letter which represents the correct answer in each problem.

① A fraction equivalent to $\frac{3}{4}$ is

    A. $\frac{5}{6}$ B. $\frac{6}{8}$ C. $\frac{35}{45}$ D. $\frac{9}{16}$

② The fraction $\frac{36}{92}$ expressed in lowest terms is

    A. $\frac{1}{2}$ B. $\frac{18}{46}$ C. $\frac{9}{23}$ D. $\frac{2}{5}$

③ The fraction $\frac{1}{8}$ expressed as a decimal is

    A. 0.12   B. 0.2   C. 0.1   D. 0.125

④ The decimal 0.95 expressed as a fraction in lowest terms is

    A. $\frac{19}{20}$ B. $\frac{9}{10}$ C. $\frac{9.5}{10}$ D. $\frac{9}{100}$

⑤ The mixed number $3\frac{1}{3}$ expressed as an improper fraction is

    A. $\frac{1}{2}$ B. $\frac{10}{3}$ C. $\frac{31}{3}$ D. $\frac{10}{9}$

⑥ The improper fraction $\frac{27}{7}$ expressed as a mixed number is

    A. $3\frac{1}{7}$ B. $27\frac{1}{7}$ C. $4\frac{6}{7}$ D. $3\frac{6}{7}$

⑦ The sum of $\frac{3}{11}$ and $\frac{7}{11}$ is

    A. $\frac{10}{11}$ B. $\frac{10}{22}$ C. $\frac{21}{121}$ D. $\frac{21}{11}$

⑧ The difference between $\frac{7}{9}$ and $\frac{2}{9}$ is

    A. $\frac{1}{7}$ B. 5   C. $\frac{5}{9}$ D. $\frac{14}{81}$

⑨ The improper fraction $\frac{24}{5}$ expressed as a decimal is

    A. 2.8   B. 4.8   C. 24.2   D. 5.2

Represent each diagram as a fraction in lowest terms and also as a decimal.

⑩

Fraction _____

Decimal _____

⑪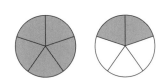

Fraction _____

Decimal _____

⑫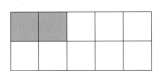

Fraction _____

Decimal _____

Write the numbers labelled A - E on the number line below as fractions and decimals.

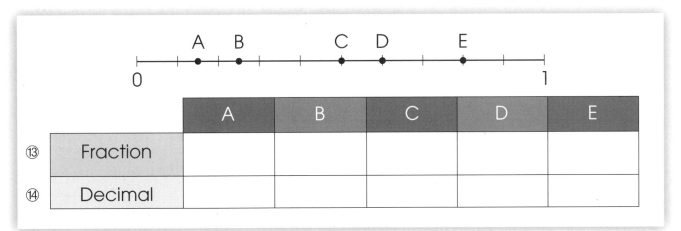

	A	B	C	D	E
⑬ Fraction					
⑭ Decimal					

Change the fractions to mixed numbers. Place the fractions on the number line below.

⑮ $\frac{15}{4}$ = _____

⑯ $\frac{3}{2}$ = _____

⑰ $\frac{17}{5}$ = _____

⑱ $\frac{19}{9}$ = _____

⑲ $\frac{4}{3}$ = _____

⑳ $\frac{7}{2}$ = _____

㉑ $\frac{14}{3}$ = _____

㉒ $\frac{25}{6}$ = _____

㉓ $\frac{35}{8}$ = _____

㉔ $\frac{7}{4}$ = _____

㉕ $\frac{13}{5}$ = _____

㉖ $\frac{24}{5}$ = _____

㉗

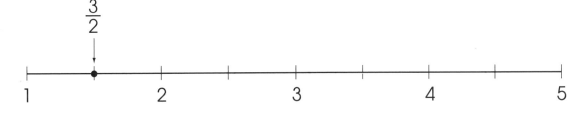

Add or subtract. Write your answers as mixed numbers in lowest terms.

㉘ $\dfrac{10}{3} - \dfrac{10}{3}$ = _____

㉙ $\dfrac{9}{2} - \dfrac{5}{2}$ = _____

㉚ $7\dfrac{1}{4} - 3\dfrac{1}{4}$ = _____

㉛ $6\dfrac{3}{8} - 5\dfrac{1}{8}$ = _____

㉜ $\dfrac{16}{5} + \dfrac{6}{5}$ = _____

㉝ $5\dfrac{1}{4} + 3\dfrac{3}{4}$ = _____

㉞ $5\dfrac{1}{4} - 4\dfrac{3}{4}$ = _____

㉟ $3\dfrac{1}{5} - 2\dfrac{3}{5}$ = _____

The chart below shows the minimum hourly wage in a number of Canadian provinces. Read the chart and answer the questions. Write the number sentences where necessary.

Province	B.C.	Alberta	Manitoba	Ontario	Quebec	PEI	Nova Scotia
Wage ($)	7.60	5.90	6.00	6.85	6.90	5.40	5.60

㊱ What is the difference between the highest and lowest wages?

_____ = _____

㊲ How much would a student working for 5 hours at minimum wage earn in

   a. Ontario? _____ = _____

   b. B.C.? _____ = _____

㊳ What is the difference between the two amounts in ㊲ ?

_____ = _____

㊴ Write the minimum wage in Quebec as

   a. a mixed number. _____

   b. an improper fraction. _____

㊵ Brenda lives in Alberta and earns $ $\dfrac{3}{4}$ per hour more than the minimum wage. How much does she earn per hour?

_____ = _____

Solve the problems. Show your work.

㊶ In 1969, Canada's population was 21.3 million and in 1994, it was 29.2 million.

    a.   Express each of these numbers as a mixed number in lowest terms.

    b.   What was the increase in Canada's population between 1969 and 1994? Express your answer as a decimal and also as a mixed number.

    c.   If this trend continues, what will the population of Canada be in 2019?

㊷ Dan is training for a Marathon race. His monthly goal is 100 km. He ran 35 km during the first week of the month.

    a.   What fraction of his monthly goal has he run? Express your answer as a proper fraction in lowest terms and as a decimal.

    b.   What distance does he still have to run during the month to achieve his goal?

    c.   What fraction of the total distance does he still have to run? Express your answer as a fraction and as a decimal.

    d.   What is the difference between the fraction of the total distance run in the first week and the fraction run during the rest of the month?

43. Mr King drinks an average of $2\frac{1}{4}$ cups of tea each day. Mrs King drinks an average of $3\frac{3}{4}$ cups per day.

    a. How many cups of tea do they drink between them each day?

    b. What is the difference between the amounts they drink per day?

    c. Change the amount Mr King drinks to a decimal. How much tea will Mr King drink per week?

    d. Change the amount Mrs King drinks to a decimal. How much tea will Mrs King drink per week?

44. Peter watches TV for $8\frac{1}{5}$ hours per week. David watches $9\frac{3}{5}$ hours and Ruth watches $7\frac{1}{5}$ hours.

    a. How much TV do they watch among them in a week?

    b. How much longer does David watch TV than Peter?

    c. How much longer does David watch TV than Ruth?

    d. Ruth's mother says that Ruth must cut down watching TV by $1\frac{3}{5}$ hours. How much TV can she watch now?

1 Operations with Whole Numbers

1. 700	2. 570	3. 800	4. 70000
5. 290	6. 90	7. 200	8. 620
9. 100	10. 300	11. 1000	12. 40
13. 6580	14. 111	15. 6753	16. 8229
17. 85	18. 2512	19. 73	

20.
```
        6 5
   5 ) 3 2 5
        3 0
        2 5
        2 5
```
21.
```
      2 9 1
  3 ) 8 7 3
      6
      2 7
      2 7
        3
        3
```
22.
```
        9 2
   8 ) 7 3 6
        7 2
        1 6
        1 6
```

23. 4833	24. 5124	25. 1065

26. 7002 + 499 = 7501   27. 984 - 578 = 406

28.
A 2	G 1	0	
5	2	C 3	0
	D 2	0	7	0
E 4		F 7	5	0
6		6	

29. 2	30. 0	31. 1	32. 0
33. 4	34. 2	35. 9 ; 9	

36. 11 - 7 = 4 ; 4
37. 12 + 12 + 2 + 2 = 28 ; Its perimeter is 28 m.
38. 66 x 60 = 3960 ; It beats 3960 times in an hour.
39. 240 ÷ 12 = 20 ; 20 x 2 = 40 ; He earns $40 per day.

Just for Fun

1a. 110 , 121 , 132   b. 108 , 120 , 132
 2. 5790 ; 4563

2 Introducing Decimals

1. $\frac{52}{100}$ 2. 0.05   3. 0.3   4. $\frac{9}{100}$

5. 7.2   6. $4\frac{1}{10}$

7.
```
  |--•--•--|--•-•-------|-------|-------|-------•---|
  0  D  C     A B                             E     1
```

8. 0.01 , 0.02 , 0.1 , 0.15 , 0.2   9. 1.05 , 1.4 , 1.45 , 1.50 , 1.54
10. 5.88 , 5.80 , 5.08 , 0.58 , 0.55 , 0.50
11. 3.2 , 2.93 , 2.9 , 2.39 , 2.3 , 2.09

12. 0.05	13. 0.10	14. 0.75	15. 0.40
16. 3.16	17. 3.70	18. T	19. F
20. T	21. T	22. F	23. F
24. 7.02	25. 3.57	26. 0.16	27. 2.35
28. 0.05	29. 0.25	30. 0.70	31. 1.15
32. 1.75	33. 2		

34. tenths ; 0.5
35. hundredths ; 0.07   36. tens ; 20
37. ones ; 3   38. hundredths ; 0.06
39. hundreds ; 100   40. 5.7

41. 0.9	42. 2.0	43. 12.3	44. 5.94
45. 2.70	46. 3.10	47. 6.01	48. <
49. <	50. >	51. >	

52a. 3 hrs. 58.5 min.   b. Yes
53. She spent $64.
54. (Suggested answers)

  a. 8 (10¢)   b. 3 (25¢) ; 1 (5¢)

55. One hundred ninety-five dollars and fifty-five cents.

Just for Fun

 ■ = 3 or 1   ♠ = 1 or 3

 ♦ = 7   ♥ = 8

3 Adding Decimals

1. 1.5	2. 10.6	3. 46.8	4. 65.0
5. 22.9	6. 13.7	7. 58.21	8. 34.23
9. 30.91	10. 107.14	11. 8.83	12. 108.10
13. 6.40	14. 326.00	15. 158.01	16. 26.23
17. 12.8	18. 6.68	19. 7.63	20. 8.23
21. 14.63	22. 7.93	23. 52.57	24. 29.15
25. 162.13	26. 811.82	27. 167.45	28. 370.42
29. 16.18	30. 115.9	31. 30.65	32. 9.09
33. 21.83	34. 21.14	35. 980	

36. 20 + 5 + 0.8 + 0.07   37. 10 + 2 + 0.9 + 0.03

38. 570.8	39. 108.64	40. $10.27	41. $11.17
42. $11.32	43. $11.14	44. $60.07	45. $71.44

46. $69.83   47. $11.17 , $11.32 , $60.07 , $71.44
48. $154.00   49. $154.00   50. 18.7   51. 24.6
52. 23.3   53. 17.4   54. + ; +
55. 5.50 + 5.50 + 3.75 + 1.2 + 1.2 = 17.15 ; $17.15
56. 6.75 + 5.9 + 6.5 + 5 = 24.15 ;
    She gets $24.15 over the 4-week period.
57. 25.2 + 22.1 + 24.8 + 28.2 = 100.3 ;
    He cycled 100.3 km during the week.

Just for Fun

  5 ; 7 ; 5

4 Subtracting Decimals

1. 0.5	2. 56.5	3. 6.3	4. 1.2
5. 28.4	6. 33.8	7. 5.04	8. 0.69
9. 3.06	10. 579.16	11. 23.71	12. 1.98
13. 5.03	14. 3.77	15. 8.27	16. 3.02
17. 11.38	18. 7.87	19. 1.82	20. 0.88
21. 0.22	22. 0.26	23. 0.81	24. 0
25. 0.06	26. 32.47	27. 26.4	28. 150.77
29. 50	30. 19.78	31. 199.4	32. 3
33. 1	34. 40	35. 9	36. 14
37. 14	38. 2.7	39. 1.8	40. 11.1
41. 18.4	42. 34.3	43. 12.6	44. 1.4
45. 8.0	46. 3.36	47. 2.4	48. 1.9
49. 2.61	50. 4.2	51. 1.23	52. 7
53. 0.6	54. 7.7	55. 7.38	56. 14.13

57. 9.46
58.
11.4	7.7	7.38	7.0	6.94
17.0	5.8	1.4	10.6	9.17
7.5	0.2	14.13	5.2	3.61
15.1	9.3	4.2	14.0	15.2
14.8	3.63	9.46	41.11	12.3
12.3	22.3	2.61	2.60	11.36
2.63	0.6	8.0	1.23	3.27

59. I
60. 35 - 32.85 ; 2.15 ; $2.15
61. 45.2 - 41.5 = 3.7 ; Sue is 3.7 kg heavier than her sister.
62. 0.55 - 0.19 = 0.36 ; The CN Tower is 0.36 km taller.
63. 12.13 - 11.87 = 0.26 ; Carl took 0.26 seconds longer.

Just for Fun

4	9	2
3	5	7
8	1	6

5 More Adding and Subtracting of Decimals

1. 19.5	2. 2	3. 6.99	4. 14
5. 10.5	6. 1.5	7. 0	8. 15
9. 10	10. 28	11. 0.5	12. 17.5
13. 10	14. 100	15. 15.45	16. 3.28
17. 8.8	18. 5.01	19. 4.69	20. 4.8
21. 109.25	22. 20.33	23. 243.6	24. 1003.8

25. 0.93   26. 100.27   27. 14.56   28. 10.66
29. $15.44   30. $73.10   31. $24.80   32. $98
33. $10.24   34. $11.52   35. 59¢   36. 33¢
37. 22¢   38. 7¢   39. 8.1   40. 1.67
41. 1.5   42. 20   43. 0.65   44. 3.44
45. 25 - 4.55 - 6.99 = 13.46 ; $13.46
46. 35 - 5.95 - 17.45 = 11.6 ; She has $11.60 left.
47. 6.50 + 19.95 + 7.50 - 2.00 = 31.95 ; Each of them spent $31.95.
48. 17.5 + 17.5 + 17.5 = 52.5 ; 20.95 + 20.95 + 6.3 = 48.2 ;
They have enough money.

Just for Fun

1¢ + 2¢ + 4¢ + 8¢ + 16¢ + 32¢ + 64¢ = 127¢ ($1.27)

6 Multiplying Decimals by Whole Numbers

1. 1   2. 32   3. 0.7   4. 0.08
5. 12   6. 9.9   7. 24.06   8. 540
9. 91.5   10. 0.1   11. 10   12. 93
13. 200.8   14. 8   15. 6.2   16. 1
17. 248   18. 1   19. 14.1   20. 10.76
21. 54.5   22. 45.29   23. 44.40   24. 65.7
25. 34.3   26. 97.6   27. 28.60   28. 59.34
29. 10.8   30. 3.92   31. 33.81   32. 1.62
33. 29.25   34. 9.66   35. 23.2   36. 506.1
37. 29.97   38. 4.56   39. 35 ; 36.4
40. 8 ; 7.4   41. 50 ; 49.05   42. 48 ; 49.38
43. 12 ; 11.25   44. 3.2 ; 2.88   45. 1.8 ; 1.53
46. 32 ; 33.76   47. 13.86   48. ✓   49. 3.09
50. 100   51. 3   52. 10   53. 100
54. 159   55. 30.9   56. 23.99 x 3 ; 71.97 ; $71.97
57. 89.50 x 4 = 358 ; The total cost is $358.
58. 2.3 x 5 = 11.5 ; He walks 11.5 km in a 5 day week.
59. 3.2 x 8 = 25.6 ; They occupy 25.6 cm.
60. 12.95 x 3 = 38.85 ; 39.99 x 2 = 79.98 ; 38.85 + 79.98 = 118.83 ;
She pays $119 altogether.

Just for Fun

444 + 44 + 4 + 4 + 4 = 500

7 Dividing Decimals by Whole Numbers

1. 0.98   2. 0.032   3. 0.75   4. 0.0092
5. 0.328   6. 0.0005   7. 0.008   8. 1.5493
9. 3.1645   10. 17.6   11. 0.12   12. 2.07
13. 0.52

14.
```
     1.15
  7) 8.05
     7
     1 0
       7
       3 5
       3 5
```
15.
```
     7.4
  9) 66.6
     63
     3 6
     3 6
```
16.
```
     10.5
  7) 73.5
     7
     3 5
     3 5
```
17.
```
     1.42
  6) 8.52
     6
     2 5
     2 4
       1 2
       1 2
```
18.
```
     0.06
  4) 0.24
     2 4
```
19.
```
     20.1
  8) 160.8
     16
        8
        8
```
20.
```
     4.03
  3) 12.09
     12
        9
        9
```
21.
```
     10.53
  5) 52.65
     5
     2 6
     2 5
       1 5
       1 5
```
22.
```
     4.55
  8) 36.4
     32
     4 4
     4 0
       4 0
       4 0
```

23.
```
     17.6
  4) 70.4
     4
     30
     28
      2 4
      2 4
```
24.
```
     2.08
  5) 10.4
     10
       40
       40
```
25.
```
     2.15
  9) 19.35
     18
      1 3
        9
        4 5
        4 5
```
26.
```
     2.3
  4) 9.2
     8
     1 2
     1 2
```
27.
```
     0.19
  3) 0.57
     3
     27
     27
```
28.
```
     2.55
  2) 5.1
     4
     1 1
     1 0
       1 0
       1 0
```
29.
```
     5.12
  7) 35.84
     35
      8
      7
      1 4
      1 4
```
30.
```
     152.1
  5) 760.5
     5
     26
     25
      10
      10
        5
        5
```
31.
```
     7.01
  5) 35.05
     35
        5
        5
```
32.
```
     1.3
  8) 10.4
     8
     2.4
     2.4
```
33.
```
     54.3
  7) 380.1
     35
     30
     28
      2 1
      2 1
```
34.
```
     125.85
  4) 503.4
     4
     10
      8
      23
      20
       3.4
       3.2
        20
        20
```
35.
```
     0.09
  5) 0.45
     45
```
36.
```
     6.53
  9) 58.77
     54
      4 7
      4 5
        27
        27
```
37.
```
     83.73
  6) 502.38
     48
     22
     18
      4 3
      4 2
        18
        18
```

38. LITTLE STARS   39. 32.5 ÷ 10 ; 3.25 ; 3.25 kg
40. 7350 ÷ 100 = 73.5 ; He travelled 73.5 km each hour.
41. 36.4 ÷ 8 = 4.55 ; Each part is 4.55 m.
42. 394 ÷ 8 = $49.25 ; Each student pays $49.25.
43. 13.5 ÷ 3 = 4.5 ; The length of each side is 4.5 cm.

Just for Fun

21 ; 34 ; 55

8 More Multiplying and Dividing of Decimals

1. 73.4   2. 0.923   3. 1.234   4. 1.21
5. 12.3   6. 120   7. 0.03   8. 10.1
9. 3.429   10. 34290   11. 125   12. 0.002
13. 4   14. 11.8   15. 4   16. 0.0125
17. 0.2   18. 635

19.
```
     23.6
  4) 94.4
     8
     14
     12
      2 4
      2 4
```
20.
```
     1.04
  7) 7.28
     7
      28
      28
```
21.
```
     15.03
  3) 45.09
     3
     15
     15
        9
        9
```
22.
```
     3.92
  x    4
    15.68
```
23.
```
     10.3
  x    7
    72.1
```
24.
```
     5.91
  x    6
    35.46
```

25.
```
    1.32
6)7.92
    6
    1 9
    1 8
      1 2
      1 2
```
26.
```
     1.9
9)17.1
   9
   8 1
   8 1
```
27.
```
    1.24
5)6.2
    5
    1 2
    1 0
      2 0
      2 0
```

28.
```
  0.47
x    8
3.76
```
29.
```
   18.2
x     9
163.8
```
30.
```
   36.7
x     2
 73.4
```

31. 10   32. 7   33. 0.17   34. 2.6
35. 27.72   36. 25.6   37. 89   38. 190
(39, 42, 44 : products < 15)
40. 15.8   41. 15.2   43. 15.5
(46, 47 quotients > 2)

45.
```
    1.4
9)12.6
    9
    3 6
    3 6
```
48.
```
    1.9
3)5.7
   3
   2 7
   2 7
```
49.
```
    1.8
6)10.8
    6
    4 8
    4 8
```

50.
```
    1.9
7)13.3
    7
    6 3
    6 3
```

51. 100   52. 10   53. 3.42   54. 2
55. 6.2   56. 9.1   57. 100   58. 10
59. 58.2 ÷ 3 = 19.4 ; $19.40
60. 19.95 x 3 = 59.85 ; 12.45 x 2 = 24.90 ; 1.25 x 10 = 12.50 ;
    59.85 + 24.90 + 12.50 = 97.25 ; She pays $97.25 altogether.
61. 12.99 x 2 = 25.98 ; 1.29 x 2 = 2.58 ; 1.49 x 2 = 2.98 ;
    25.98 + 2.58 + 2.98 = 31.54 ; 31.54 ÷ 5 = 6.308 ;
    They must pay $6.31 each.
62. 29.4 ÷ 3 = 9.8 ; 39.5 ÷ 5 = 7.9 ;
    A 5 kg bag for $39.5 is the better buy.

Just for Fun

0.5

Midway Review

1. 18.95   2. 11.76   3. 67.2   4. 1.05
5. 16.26   6. 0.62   7. 209.04   8. 3.2
9. 954.1   10. 14.59   11. 968.69   12. 149.5
13. 54.19   14. 95.31   15. 520 ; 5.2 16. 7 ; 0.07
17. 1.2 ; 0.012 18. 7.5 ; 0.75 19. 0.3 ; 0.03 20. 8 ; 80
21. 150 ; 1500 22. D   23. C   24. C
25. C   26. B   27. D   28. B
29. C   30. A   31. B   32. B
33. C   34. C   35. 9.0 + 3.2 + 3.2 = 15.4 ; 15.4
36. 20 x 15.4 = 308 ; The total cost is $308.
37. 9 + 3.2 + 9 + 3.2 = 24.4 ; The perimeter is 24.4 m.
38. 9 x 3.2 = 28.8 ; The area is 28.8 m².
39a. New length = 9.0 x 2 = 18.0 ; New width = 3.2 x 2 = 6.4 ;
     18.0 + 18.0 + 6.4 + 6.4 = 48.8 = 24.4 x 2 ;
     The perimeter is doubled as well.
  b. 9 x 2 x 3.2 x 2 = 9 x 3.2 x 2 x 2 = 28.8 x 4 ;
     The area is 4 times larger than before.

9 Introducing Fractions

1. $\frac{1}{6}$ 2. $\frac{1}{3}$ 3. $\frac{2}{3}$ 4. $\frac{5}{6}$
5. $\frac{1}{6}$ 6. $\frac{4}{6}=\frac{2}{3}$ 7. $\frac{5}{8}$ 8. $\frac{6}{16}=\frac{3}{8}$
9. $\frac{3}{8}$ 10. $\frac{1}{4}$
11.   12.   13.

14.   15.   16.
17.
```
 1  1        2  1          4  9
20 10        5  2          5  10
0                                1
```
18. $\frac{5}{9}$ 19. $\frac{5}{8}$ 20. $\frac{8}{11}$
21.   22.   23.
24. 5   25. 12   26. 6   27. 2
28. 2   29. 4   30. $\frac{3}{4}$ 31. $\frac{1}{3}$
32. $\frac{1}{2}$ 33. $\frac{2}{3}$ 34. $\frac{3}{8}$ 35. $\frac{4}{5}$
36. (Suggested answers) $\frac{1}{8}$; $\frac{1}{4}$; $\frac{1}{3}$
37a. $\frac{35}{100}=\frac{7}{20}$ b. $\frac{60}{100}=\frac{3}{5}$ 38. $\frac{3}{24}=\frac{1}{8}$ 39. $\frac{2}{8}=\frac{1}{4}$
40. $\frac{50}{250}=\frac{1}{5}$ 41. $\frac{1}{3}$ 42. $\frac{21}{26}$ 43. $\frac{3}{5}$
44. $\frac{5}{12}$ 45. $\frac{12}{16}=\frac{3}{4}$ 46a. $\frac{87}{100}$ b. $\frac{13}{100}$

Just for Fun

1. $\frac{1}{16}$; $\frac{1}{32}$; $\frac{1}{64}$ 2. No

10 Equivalent Fractions and Ordering of Fractions

1. 25   2. $\frac{25}{77}$ 3. 15   4. 75
5. 2   6.   7. $\frac{5}{6}$ 8. $\frac{1}{2}$
9. $\frac{2}{11}$ 10. $\frac{3}{7}$ 11. $\frac{1}{4}$ 12. $\frac{2}{3}$
13. $\frac{3}{4}$ 14. $\frac{1}{3}$ 15. $\frac{1}{6}$ 16. $\frac{2}{3}$
17. $\frac{8}{21}$ 18. $\frac{11}{15}$ 19. $\frac{1}{10}<\frac{1}{5}<\frac{1}{2}<\frac{3}{5}<\frac{7}{10}<\frac{4}{5}$
20. $\frac{1}{4}<\frac{1}{3}<\frac{2}{4}<\frac{2}{3}<\frac{3}{4}$ 21. T   22. F
23. T   24. F   25. 3 ; 12   26. 5 ; 2
27. 2 ; 4   28. 55 ; 4   29. $\frac{2}{16}$; $\frac{3}{24}$; $\frac{4}{32}$
30. $\frac{4}{6}$; $\frac{6}{9}$; $\frac{8}{12}$ 31. $\frac{2}{8}$; $\frac{3}{12}$; $\frac{4}{16}$ 32. $\frac{10}{14}$; $\frac{15}{21}$; $\frac{20}{28}$
33. $\frac{7}{8}>\frac{3}{4}>\frac{5}{6}>\frac{1}{2}>\frac{3}{8}>\frac{1}{4}>\frac{3}{16}$
34. $\frac{5}{18}>\frac{13}{3}>\frac{2}{3}>\frac{1}{2}>\frac{7}{18}>\frac{1}{3}>\frac{1}{6}$
35. <   36. =   37. >   38. <
39. <   40. <   41. $\frac{3}{4}$ 42. $\frac{3}{5}$
43. $\frac{5}{6}$ 44. $\frac{4}{9}$ 45. $\frac{7}{9}$ 46. $\frac{6}{7}$
47. $\frac{200}{450}$; $\frac{75}{125}$; $\frac{15}{20}$; $\frac{14}{18}$; $\frac{45}{54}$; $\frac{150}{175}$
48. 14 ; 14   49. 8 ; 8   50. 88 ; 88
51. Nadine : $\frac{9}{12}=\frac{27}{36}$; Danielle : $\frac{14}{18}=\frac{28}{36}$;
    Danielle has the better mark.
52a. $\frac{682}{5421}$; $\frac{1583}{8474}$ b. Increasing
  c. $\frac{512}{5421}$; $\frac{542}{8474}$ d. Decreasing

Just for Fun

$\frac{1}{16}$; $\frac{1}{25}$; $\frac{1}{36}$

11 Adding Fractions with the Same Denominator

1. 1   2. 1   3. $\frac{2}{3}$ 4. $\frac{2}{5}$

5. $\frac{5}{9}$ 6. $\frac{4}{7}$ 7. $\frac{4}{5}$ 8. 1

9. 1   10. $\frac{8}{9}$ 11. $\frac{11}{13}$ 12. $\frac{8}{11}$

13. $\frac{7}{8}$ 14. $\frac{13}{20}$ 15. $\frac{9}{17}$ 16. $\frac{9}{19}$

17. $\frac{21}{25}$ 18. $\frac{10}{12}=\frac{5}{6}$ 19. $\frac{17}{21}$ 20. $\frac{8}{15}$

21. $\frac{6}{16}=\frac{3}{8}$ 22. $\frac{2}{4}=\frac{1}{2}$ 23. $\frac{12}{18}=\frac{2}{3}$ 24. $\frac{22}{23}$

25. $\frac{4}{6}=\frac{2}{3}$ 26. $\frac{25}{27}$ 27. $\frac{13}{20}$ 28. $\frac{12}{15}=\frac{4}{5}$

29. $\frac{3}{9}=\frac{1}{3}$ 30. $\frac{12}{14}=\frac{6}{7}$ 31. $\frac{6}{8}=\frac{3}{4}$ 32. $\frac{6}{10}=\frac{3}{5}$

33. $\frac{8}{16}=\frac{1}{2}$ 34. $\frac{6}{12}=\frac{1}{2}$ 35. $\frac{4}{20}=\frac{1}{5}$ 36. $\frac{2}{6}=\frac{1}{3}$

37. $\frac{4}{7}$ 38. $\frac{3}{18}=\frac{1}{6}$ 39. $\frac{6}{24}=\frac{1}{4}$ 40. $\frac{8}{32}=\frac{1}{4}$

41. 1   42. 1

43. $\frac{4}{8}=\frac{1}{2}$ 44. $\frac{1}{3}+\frac{2}{3}=1$

45. $\frac{3}{6}+\frac{1}{6}=\frac{4}{6}=\frac{2}{3}$ 46. $\frac{1}{4}+\frac{1}{4}=\frac{2}{4}=\frac{1}{2}$

47. $\frac{1}{3}+\frac{2}{3}=1$ 48. $\frac{1}{5}+\frac{2}{5}=\frac{3}{5}$

49. $\frac{2}{7}$ 50. $\frac{1}{11}$ 51. $\frac{5}{6}$ 52. $\frac{7}{8}$

53. $\frac{1}{4}$ 54. $\frac{1}{8}$ 55. $\frac{1}{15}$ 56. $\frac{1}{10}$

57. $\frac{11}{20}$ 58. $\frac{5}{12}$ 59. $\frac{11}{25}$ 60. $\frac{2}{9}$

61. $\frac{1}{4}+\frac{1}{4}+\frac{1}{4}=\frac{3}{4}$

62a. $\frac{2}{6}+\frac{2}{6}+\frac{1}{6}=\frac{5}{6}$; They eat $\frac{5}{6}$ pizza.

b. $\frac{5}{6}<1$; There is some pizza left.

63a. $\frac{5}{8}+\frac{1}{8}=\frac{6}{8}=\frac{3}{4}$; She needs $\frac{3}{4}$ m altogether.

b. $\frac{3}{4}<1$; She will have enough ribbon.

64a. $\frac{3}{10}+\frac{1}{10}=\frac{4}{10}=\frac{2}{5}$; She has spent $\frac{2}{5}$ of her allowance.

b. $\frac{2}{5}+\frac{3}{5}=1$; She has $\frac{3}{5}$ left.

Just for Fun

$\frac{8}{15}$	$\frac{1}{15}$	$\frac{6}{15}$
$\frac{3}{15}$	$\frac{5}{15}$	$\frac{7}{15}$
$\frac{4}{15}$	$\frac{9}{15}$	$\frac{2}{15}$

12 Improper Fractions and Mixed Numbers

1. $2\frac{1}{7}$ 2. $\frac{27}{8}$ 3. $3\frac{2}{3}$ 4. $\frac{45}{4}$

5. $1\frac{2}{5}$ 6. $\frac{4}{7};\frac{5}{20};\frac{7}{9};\frac{11}{12}$

7. $\frac{9}{9};\frac{25}{20};\frac{15}{8};\frac{16}{7}$ 8. $3\frac{3}{10};3\frac{1}{2};1\frac{5}{20};1\frac{2}{5}$

9. $2\frac{2}{3};\frac{8}{3}$ 10. $1\frac{1}{6};\frac{7}{6}$

11.
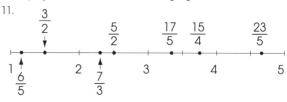

12. $\frac{8}{6}=\frac{4}{3}$ 13. $\frac{13}{6}$ 14. $\frac{15}{6}=\frac{5}{2}$ 15. $\frac{16}{6}=\frac{8}{3}$

16. $\frac{20}{6};\frac{10}{3}$ 17. $\frac{23}{6}$ 18. $\frac{15}{4}>\frac{7}{2}>\frac{7}{3}>\frac{9}{4}>\frac{5}{3}$

19. $\frac{17}{2}>\frac{17}{3}>\frac{17}{4}>\frac{17}{5}>\frac{17}{6}$ 20. $\frac{23}{6};\frac{19}{6};\frac{7}{2}$

21. $\frac{60}{7};\frac{49}{6};\frac{25}{3}$

22.
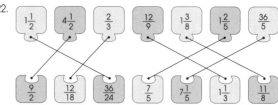

23a. $2\frac{1}{2}$ b. $\frac{5}{2}$ 24. 9

25. $1\frac{3}{5}$ 26. 9

27. False. Since $\frac{15}{4}=3\frac{3}{4}$, $\frac{13}{3}=4\frac{1}{3}$; So $\frac{13}{3}>\frac{15}{4}$

Just for Fun

56

13 Adding Improper Fractions and Mixed Numbers

1. 2   2. 3   3. 5   4. 3

5. 7   6. 3   7. 6   8. 7

9. 3   10. 2   11. 2   12. 3

13. 4   14. 2   15. $2\frac{1}{4}$ 16. $6\frac{3}{5}$

17. $3\frac{2}{5}$ 18. $5\frac{1}{2}$ 19. $3\frac{2}{5}$ 20. $3\frac{1}{2}$

21. $1\frac{1}{2}$ 22. $4\frac{1}{3}$ 23. $1\frac{3}{5}$ 24. $2\frac{7}{8}$

25. $3\frac{1}{4}$ 26. 2   27. $4\frac{3}{4}$ 28. $2\frac{1}{3}$

29. $9\frac{2}{5}$ 30. 6   31. $\frac{3}{4}$ 32. $\frac{5}{8}$

33. $1\frac{4}{5}$ 34. $1\frac{1}{2}$ 35. $\frac{1}{2}$ 36. $\frac{3}{5}$

37. $\frac{2}{3}$ 38. $\frac{7}{6}$ 39. $3\frac{1}{5}$ 40. $\frac{3}{4}$

41. T   42. T   43. F   44. T

45. T   46. F   47. T   48. F

50, 51, 55 < 3.   49. $3\frac{1}{3}$ 52. $3\frac{1}{2}$

53. $3\frac{1}{2}$ 54. $3\frac{1}{5}$ 56. $3\frac{5}{9}$

57. $1\frac{1}{4}+2\frac{1}{4}+1\frac{3}{4}=5\frac{1}{4}$; They eat $5\frac{1}{4}$ cans of food per week.

58. $45\frac{3}{8}+2\frac{1}{8}=47\frac{1}{2}$; The new selling price is $47\frac{1}{2}$ ¢.